PRAYER STATIONS ™

PRAYER STATIONS ™

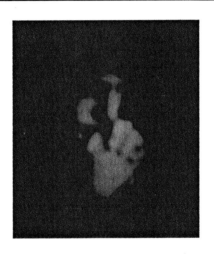

*A Guide to Focused Prayer
And Intercession*

JOURNAL

Byron Ravenell
Georgia M. Hood

Prayer Station Vissionaries:
>   Byron Ravenell
>   Georgia Hood

Bibles Used:
King James Version (KJV)
New King James Version (NKJV)
>   Scripture taken from the New King James Version. Copyright © 1979, 1980, 1982 by Thomas Nelson, Inc. Used by permission. All rights reserved.

Good News Bible (GNB)
>   Scripture taken from the Today's English Version—Second Edition © 1992
>   Old Testament ©American Bible Society 1976, 1992
>   New Testament ©American Bible Society 1966, 1971, 1976, 1992
>   Maps: ©United Bible Societies 1976 by Thomas Nelson, Inc.

Copyright © 2003 by Byron Ravenell & Georgia M. Hood

ISBN :   Hardcover   1-4134-3126-7
            Softcover   1-4134-3125-9

All rights reserved. No part of this book may be reproduced or transmitted in any form or by any means, electronic or mechanical, including photocopying, recording, or by any information storage and retrieval system, without permission in writing from the copyright owner.

This book was printed in the United States of America.

To order additional copies of this book, contact:
Xlibris Corporation
1-888-795-4274
www.Xlibris.com
Orders@Xlibris.com
20924

CONTENTS

Theme Song 9
The Birthing of Prayer Stations 11
Acknowledgements 15
Vision 17
Introduction 19

Prayer Stations

Prayer Station I Praise and Worship 29
Prayer Station II Family 39
Prayer Station III Children 47
Prayer Station IV Finance 57
Prayer Station V Healing 67
Prayer Station VI Binding Satan 75
Prayer Station VII Leadership 85
Prayer Station VIII Unity 93
Prayer Station IX Prisoners/Captives 103
Prayer Station X Bondage 111
Prayer Station XI Addiction 119
Prayer Station XII Salvation 127

Prayer Stations "On the Run"

Bibliography 145
Summary 147
Author biography—Byron R. Ravenell 149
Author Biography—Georgia M. Hood 151

Prayer Stations

"A Call to Prayer"

THEME SONG

He wants to open the door
He wants to give you more
There's nothing He cannot do for you
So let Him see you through
He gave His only Son
So that we can freely come
God is waiting for you at Prayer Stations

THE BIRTHING OF PRAYER STATIONS
GOD'S VISION

"Again I say to you, That if two of you shall agree on earth as touching anything that they shall ask, it shall be done for them of my Father which is in Heaven. For where two or three are gathered together in my name, there am I in the midst of them."—Matthew 18:19-20.

Prayer Stations are a gift and vision from God, who inspired Byron Ravenell and Georgia Hood to write it down and carry it to the nations. The two had never met before, but shared two things in common; they both were full of the Holy Ghost and attended prayer services at the same location, Samaritan Baptist Church in Trenton, New Jersey.

Byron Ravenell was the Minister of Music of Samaritan Baptist church. Georgia Hood, an evangelist at Grace Cathedral Fellowship Ministries, had begun a City Wide Women's Prayer Meeting that met at Samaritan on the first and third Saturdays of each month. God spoke to Evangelist Hood and said, "go tell the Ravenells that I have need of this church." After speaking those words to Evangelist Mary Ravenell, she responded, "and I have need of Him." There was an automatic spontaneity and a commitment to move forward. The prayer started on the first Saturday of November 2000. God had the power of synergy in mind, to birth a vision that would take two to stand in agreement and run with it.

God was doing wonderful things through the prayer meetings and the Holy Spirit began to move in a new direction at Samaritan Baptist Church. Beginning January 2001, Evangelist Ravenell testified that services were never the same. Yet God still wanted to do more.

One Saturday morning at the prayer meeting, Evangelist Hood asked the women to share with the group what was in their hearts and what they want the group to pray for. The women all shared their concerns and there were many common themes; their families, children, finance, health and so forth. One woman wept when she shared her concern about abuse towards children. She touched the hearts of the entire group, and individuals ran to hug her as she finished her testimony. Then Evangelist Hood asked the women to get together with those who had the same concerns as they did, and pray, touching and agreeing. There was love and communion in the room—something new—something different. There was a birthing-taking place and the manifestation of the Holy Spirit was in the room at this prayer service. The vision of Prayer Stations was being birth in the midst. Spiritual birth is delivered through the midwives of prayer.

At the same time, the Lord began to deal with Byron to approach the Pastor about having a miracle victory service. God spoke into his spirit that He was bored at the mundane requests that were being made in prayer to an Awesome God who is capable of blessing His people more exceedingly abundantly, if only we would allow Him to do so. The Pastor immediately agreed to the service. Leading up to the Saturday miracle service, the church was in continuous prayer and fasting, some members shut themselves in the church for 3 days and 2 nights.

The Lord gave Byron the vision of "prayer stations," and led him to set up prayer stations at specific locations throughout the church, which corresponded with the needs that the women had already testified of. These prayer stations were on 24x18 cardboard paper, written in no particular format. Byron believed he was being led to help individuals at Samaritan who had similar prayer requests to come together and bombard heaven with the their petitions, as well as be in agreement with one another as the Scripture says in Matthew 18:19. To his surprise it was more than that.

The miracle service was a success. God showed Himself in a way that only He could and He received all the Glory. The Holy Spirit led the Pastor to keep the prayer stations hanging in the sanctuary after the miracle service.

When Evangelist Hood came to the Women's Prayer meeting the following Saturday, The Lord arrested her spirit immediately and began to show her that the prayer stations was for the "nations," not just for Samaritan Baptist Church. The Lord began to show greater dimensions about the prayer stations to her spirit. The Holy Spirit moved on her to immediately add a station on "Praise and Worship" and "Binding Satan" and Evangelist Hood ensured that they were erected on cardboard paper as the others. Evangelist Hood asked Pastor Ravenell for permission to augment the vision to what the Lord was showing her, and he agreed. The Lord showed Evangelist Hood that Prayer Stations was for the nations, not just for Samaritan Baptist Church in Trenton, New Jersey.

Pastor Joseph Ravenell was the mediator of the vision until Byron and Georgia met. Finally, Byron and Georgia were introduced to each other. She began to share with him what the Lord was birthing in her in order for prayer stations to serve the nations. From that point on they came into agreement and allowed God to minister to them as they wrote down the worldwide vision. The Prayer Stations were further developed as the two became one in the vision of The Prayer Stations.

There were specific requests the Lord made that were to be included in the Prayer Stations (Phase II):

1. God supernaturally showed the format for the new banners.
2. Banners Praise and Worship, Binding Satan and Salvation were added.
3. Add scriptures to each prayer station.
4. Each Prayer Station should be numbered—starting with Praise and Worship and ending with the Salvation banner—for God is a God of order.

5. Use *focal points* that are soul stirring and reflective. Use focal points that will cause the one praying to deal with his own issues *first* and be healed. Use focal points that will provoke the sinner to repentance.
6. A piece of the armor in Ephesians 6:11-18 should be at the bottom of each prayer station (the believer is to put on the whole armor of God in praying the word).
7. Add a Salvation Prayer Station with the scriptures written out so that an unbeliever could be lead to Christ without a Bible.
8. Specific material and hardware to be used for the banners.
9. Last but not least—an angle was added to the stations with an emphasis of sounding the trumpet as a "call to prayer."

As the team rolled out the new silk banners for the first time, a supernatural move of God took place at Prayer Station XII. A supernatural light began to shoot through the banner from left to right leaving no parts of the banner untouched. It was as if the hand of God was sealing the work. The presence of the Almighty God came down in our midst—it was a visitation from God, and it was awesome.

Had God not brought Byron and Georgia together, the Prayer Stations would not be what they are today. God has charged the visionaries to relay His message of focused prayer and intercession to the nations.

The move of God is supernatural at each station and miracles, signs and wonders are being performed as individuals by faith meet the Lord at Prayer Stations. There are testimonies of healing, deliverance, salvation, restoration and financial break through. Children also are praying the stations and being blessed. What a charismatic move of God!

God loves us so much that He has given us yet another guide to receiving what He has for His people. To God be the glory.

ACKNOWLEDGEMENTS

The woman of God who has most inspired us through her prayer life is Evangelist Mary Ravenell. She is a woman of prayer and integrity, and is fervent in the things of God. The law of kindness also is written in her heart.

"Her children arise up, and call her blessed; her husband also, and he praiseth her" (Proverbs 31:28). Our confidante and friend!

A special thanks to Bishop Jerome S. Wilcox and Pastor Joseph Ravenell, who are the shepherds and Bishops of our souls. Thanks to Evangelist Katherine Johnson who the Holy Spirit inspired to put the 1st phase of the prayer stations on cardboard paper. To Cynthia Lewis our silk banner designer of phase II—both women are filled with the Spirit of God, in wisdom, in understanding, in knowledge and in all manner of workmanship (Exodus 35:31-33). To our editors, Dr. Paulette Wilson, Rekema Stokes and Dana Ross.

To God be the glory!

PRAYER STATIONS

VISION

It is our vision that prayer revival will break forth throughout the body of Christ as a result of believers praying the Word of God. That miracles, signs, and wonders will be evident as souls are delivered and set free by the power of God as they meet the Holy Spirit at each Prayer Station.

That Prayer Station banners will be in every house of worship, and that this prayer journal will be in the hands of every believer.

It is our desire that each believer will be blessed as they pray the will of God in their lives and the lives of others!

Salvation is our number one priority—that souls will be made whole.

Vision Scripture

Acts 4:29-32 (KJV)

And now, Lord, behold their threatening: and grant unto thy servants, that with all boldness they may speak thy word, By stretching forth thine hand to heal; and that signs and wonders may be done by the name of thy holy child Jesus. And when they had prayed, the place was shaken were they were assembled together; and they were all filled with the Holy Ghost, and they spake the word of God with boldness. And the multitude of them that believed were of one heart and of one soul:

INTRODUCTION

What is prayer?

In order to be effective in prayer we must first understand what it is.

Prayer is a request, petition or entreaty. How a request is received and responded to depends on the type of relationship between the one making the request and the one receiving it. The parent to child relationship is the most important one that exists. No love is comparable to that of the parent and the child. So it is with the relationship with God and mankind. When Jesus Christ gives us the model for prayer in the New Testament, (Matthew 6:9-13 and Luke 11:2-4 KJV) he begins with "Our Father." Once we realize and accept this truth, we can confidently go to God in prayer.

The Three Dimensions of Prayer

Prayer is asking, seeking and knocking, three-dimensional. The first letters in *A*sk, *S*eek and *K*nock spells "ASK"—Prayer is simply *Asking* (petitioning) the Father, *Seeking* (communion) Him, and *Knocking* (interceding) for others. Prayer is talking with God. More than just asking, it is confession, adoration, thanksgiving, and fellowship with God.

Not praying is considered a sin for it is the foundation for a successful Christian life (1 Samuel 12:23). When the believer prays he should follow the model that Jesus gave his disciples and include in Jesus' name (Matthew 6:9-15; John 14:14).

Matthew 7:7-8—"Ask, and it shall be given you; seek, and ye shall find; knock, and it shall be opened unto you: For every one that asketh receiveth; and he that seeketh findeth; and to him that knocketh it shall be opened."

What is a Station?

A station is a place where one stands or is located; an assigned post or location, for example, a service or gas station serves two purposes. It is the place where oil companies know to bring their products to provide service such as gasoline, motor oil, air filters, etc. It is also the place where consumers know to bring their automobile to receive services such as refueling, oil change, and check ups. A train or bus station serves similar purposes. Vehicles go to terminals in order to provide transportation to various locations for passengers. Passengers go to the stations looking for and expecting transportation to their specific destination.

What is a Prayer Station?

Just as the pool of Bethesda (John 5:2-4) was a place where the sick came to be healed, when an angel came to trouble the waters, so is the vision of Prayer Stations.

A Prayer Station is a designated location where believers go, expecting to receive results from God the Father in the name of Jesus Christ, *in the lives of both themselves and others.* It also serves as a location where the power of agreement is activated by faith.

Intercession

Intercession is the prayer of intervention made on behalf of someone with a particular need. When the believer intercedes he enters into his priestly anointing and provides a gateway by standing in the gap for God's divine will and purpose.

The Holy Spirit intercedes through the believer. *The Holy Spirit prays with classified information, for He prays according to the will of God.*

The biblical view of intercession describes Christ's intervention on behalf of believer's weaknesses and temptations, which is our example. Christ is continually and actively interceding on our behalf. The entire body of Christ has been called to intercede.

Paul says it profoundly, "My little children, of whom I travail in birth again until Christ be formed in you" (Galatians 4:19, KJV).

"Wherefore he is able also to save them to the uttermost that come unto God by him, seeing he ever liveth to make intercession for them" (Hebrews 7:25).

Fasting and Prayer

To fast means to intentionally abstain from food for a specified amount of time and a particular purpose. Fasting is key to encountering results in the life of the believer, the lives of others, the community, church and nations that are under the attack of Satan. Fasting also allows the believer's spirit to be sensitive to the moving of God. It positions the believer to exercise his spiritual authority and the forces of Satan must come under subjection to the will of God.

"Is not this the fast that I have chosen? To loose the bands of wickedness, to undo the heavy burdens and to let the oppressed go free, and that ye break every yoke?" (Isaiah 58:6 KJV).

Design of each Prayer Station:

1. The Prayer Stations are overshadowed by the name of Jesus, which is the name above every name (Philippians 2:9-11).

2. Each Prayer Station depicts one of the Old Testament names of God, displaying his power, character and his attributes (Exodus 6:2-3). A *brief* description is given in this book regarding the name at each station.
3. Each Prayer Station has a unique name which is shown under the Prayer Station Number. There are 12 Prayer Stations (see table of contents).
4. The angel symbolizes "a call to prayer."
5. The Prayer Stations list specific areas that concern humanity (*focal points*), and are designed to keep the prayer warrior focused while praying and interceding. The focal points are relative to the Prayer Station name.
6. The very last line of Prayer Stations 2-11 identifies a piece of the armor listed in Ephesians 6:11-18. After the believer has prayed the entire vision, he has fully dressed himself in the whole armor of God. A *brief* description is given in this book about the armor at each station.
7. At Prayer Station XII, you will be able to lead an unbeliever to Christ without your bible, for all the necessary scriptures are written for your aid. This is the only station that does not list a piece of the whole armor of God. At this station, the believer stands full clothed and ready to do battle with the enemy to recover all that has been stolen.

Focal Point Reading

Lists of focal point scriptures are listed below each prayer station so that the believer can pray effectively the Word of God.

"Focal Points" are specific areas that concern humanity and are listed in the body of the prayer stations and are *relative to the prayer station name*. Focal points are designed to allow the believer to deal with interpersonal conflict as well as intercede for others. Focal points take the prayer warrior outside of the box into praying beyond the normal scope of things. Focal points motivate the believer to be offensive towards the enemy in initiating an aggressive attack.

Prayer Station I, (Praise and Worship) is quite unique and has focal points that lead the believer into worship. It builds the believers faith to receive from God and know that God can do anything.

Focal points can be used also on a professional level in counseling sessions, and the dynamics of teams.

Written Journal

There is a section below each Prayer Station for your written journal.

Reflections

When you reflect on what you have heard, it causes you to think about how it has impacted your heart. What changes are you willing to make, or what changes have you made as a result of reflecting? The only way we can be of greatest use to God and our fellow man is to let God take us through the cracks and crevices of our own character.

Write down your reflections as you take this journey with the Lord.

As you visit each Prayer Station reflect and let the Lord bless your life. You will find that you will be most productive at Prayer Station XII when you have wrestled and conquered some issues along the way.

Prayer Request (Petition)

When someone wants to make changes in judicial procedures that affect communities or society in any way, they sometimes write a petition and have individuals sign to validate the petition. That enables the one in authority to make a decision based on the support (evidence/signatures) behind the petition.

Likewise, when you have a particular petition before God, write it down and authenticate it with scripture. God is the one in authority to answer your prayers. When His Word is prayed He will back it up. "God is not a man, that he should lie; neither the son of man, that he should repent: hath he said, and shall he not do it? Or hath he spoken, and shall he not make it good?" (Numbers 23:19, KJV).

When scriptures are lined up with your praying it builds up your faith to receive from God. Also, when you ensure that your petition is His will for your life, your prayers *will be* answered. Pray with fervency as though you already possess your promise from the Lord.

"And this is the confidence that we have in him, that, if we *ask* anything according to *His will*, he heareth us. And if we know that he hear us, whatsoever we *ask*, we know that we have the petitions that we desired of him" (1 John 5:14-15, KJV).

Adding scripture to your prayers is not an easy task, for you must be sure that the scripture you select is what God intends for your life.

The Apostle Paul wrote down his prayers to the churches and received great results and it continues in us.

Read the following:

Ephesians 1:16 -19
Ephesians 3:14 -19
Colossians 1:9 -14

1 Thessalonians 3:11-13
1 Thessalonians 5:23-24

Insight to Answered Prayer

- Confession of sin — Psalm 66:18
- Abide in Christ — John 15:7
- Ask in faith — Mark 11:24
- Pure motives — James 4:3
- Honor Partner in marriage — 1 Peter 3:7
- Obedience to God's Word — 1 John 3:22
- Will of God — 1 John 5:14

When God answers your prayer, write the date down and have a victory party and don't forget to invite the Master.

"And he spake a parable unto them to this end, that men ought always to pray, and not to faint" (Luke 18:1 KJV).

This is your guide to focused prayer!

Prayer Stations

PRAISE AND WORSHIP

PRAYER STATION I

"O Lord, thou art my God; I will exalt thee, I will praise thy name; for thou hast done wonderful things; thy counsels of old are faithfulness and truth."
(Isaiah 25:1 KJV)

JESUS

Jehovah Elohim
The Lord Is God
Deuteronomy 10:17

Prayer Station I

Praise and Worship

Psalm 66, 113, 145

Hallow His Name
Holy—Love—Righteous
Faithful—Justice—Mercy
Gracious—Long-suffering—Humble
Goodness—Truth—Forgiving
Omniscience—Omnipotence
Omnipresence—Immutable
Infinite—Wisdom—His Glory
Creator—The Word
Potentate
King of kings—Lord of lords
Majesty—Worthy—Exalted
Alpha—Omega
New Covenant
Atonement—Redemption
Father—Son—Holy Spirit

The Whole Armor—Ephesians 6:11-18

Prayer Station I—Praise and Worship

It is by no mistake that Praise and Worship is the first Prayer Station. God is Almighty and Self-Existing. Throughout the scriptures, up to the present day, God has shown himself to the world through His many acts, beginning with His creation (Genesis 1:1).

Psalms 145 accurately demonstrates to the believer why praise is in order. Verse 10 says, *"All Your works shall praise You, O Lord, and your saints shall bless You"* (NKJV). The book of Revelation comes to a close with a command to *worship* him that made heaven and earth and the sea, and the fountains of waters (Revelation 14:7).

When we *praise* God, we realize and acknowledge who He is, what he has done, and what He is going to do. *Worship* is the outward expression of how we inwardly feel about God—it is a posture of the heart and is motivated by what we know and believe about Him. Worship is in spirit and in truth.

When we praise and worship, we realize and acknowledge who He is, what he has done, and what He is capable of. It helps our belief that our prayers are being heard. Because of God's capabilities and love for us, He will do what is best.

Primary Names of God—Exodus 3:13

There are three primary names of God: Elohim (God), Jehovah or Yahweh (usually printed as Lord in the KJV), and Adonai (Lord). Each of these names emphasizes a different aspect of the nature of God. (Nelson Study Bible KJV, p105)

Prior to Exodus 6:3, Men knew God by His powerful name "God Almighty" (El Shaddai). The Almighty, the Powerful One or the Mighty One (God) (Genesis 17:1-3). (The Hebrew-Greek Key Word Study Bible, p1666)

Elohim (God)—Genesis 2:4

God with a capital "G" and a small "od" is the name Elohim. The name mean "God." This name reflects God's divine strength and creative power. Elohim also means "something or someone that is worshiped." God told Israel that He was the only true and living God, the only Elohim to be worshiped (Exodus 20:3-6).

God is pleased when His creatures worship Him the Creator.

Jehovah or Yahweh (LORD)—Genesis 2:4

It was after the birth of Enos that "then began men to call upon the name of the LORD:" (Genesis 4:26). Before that time man had such an intimate relationship with God in His presence that there was no need to call upon Him by name.

At Exodus 3:14, the significance of God's name is given, "I AM THAT I AM." I AM THAT I AM, should be translated, "I am He who is," or "I am He who exists." This name reveals that God is self-existent especially in relations to humanity. To the Hebrew it means further that God not only exist but also is an active God. Therefore, God is the self-existent God who is active in the lives of His people.

Exodus 6:3, "And God spake unto Moses, and said unto him, I am the LORD: And I appeared unto Abraham, unto Isaac, and unto Jacob, by the name of God Almighty, but by my name JEHOVAH was I not known to them."

God introduces Himself to man (Moses) as Jehovah at this point in scripture (Exodus 6:3). Jehovah is the covenant name of God most prominently known in connection with His relationship with the nation of Israel. Jehovah is a Holy God full of glory and majesty. Fire often symbolizes his holiness, as that displayed at the burning bush. Jehovah expresses the "I AM THAT I AM" of God, his self-existence.

This name Jehovah also speaks of His hatred of sin in Genesis 6:3-7, Israel's redeemer in Exodus 6:6, a God of war in Exodus 15:3, God's holiness in Leviticus 11:44, and His graciousness in providing redemption for all of mankind in Isaiah 53:1,5,6,10.

There is no god like JEHOVAH.

Jehovah Elohim (The Lord is God)

Genesis 2:4 is the first mention of the name *Jehovah Elohim* (LORD God), "In the day that Jehovah Elohim made the earth and heavens."

All the compound names of Jehovah reveal His holiness, power, character, attributes and His sovereignty. God uses this name (Jehovah) to introduce Himself in various ways to humanity.

Worship

Jesus told the Samaritan women in John 4:24, "God is a Spirit: and they that worship him must worship him in spirit and in truth." To worship God you must be "in spirit," you must be born again. The second component is "in truth." To worship God you must know truth about Him. What does the word say about Him and what do you believe. When you worship God you speak truth about Him. Say what you know and know what you say! Worship is total focus on God.

The Armor

At this station the believer is encouraged to put on the whole armor of God (Ephesians 6:11-18). This scripture starts with standing (v11), and ends with praying (v18). Most of the metaphorical images used in this passage are taken from Isaiah 11:5, 52:7, and 59:16-17.

Prayer is one of the most powerful weapons used in the believer's warfare against sin and should be offered up for all the saints.

The believer's strategy against the enemy is to "stand" (stand against or to withstand) against his schemes fully dressed with specific armor to protect themselves. The believer is to be in a standing position holding the ground (territory) which Christ has already conquered for the Church.

This warfare is not against flesh or blood, (physical), but against Satan and his evil forces (spiritual). The heavenly realm is their spear of activity. Satan will be cast out of the heavens in the middle of the tribulation period (Revelations 12:9-10). Until that time he (Satan) is trying to rob believers of their spiritual blessings in heavenly places in Christ Jesus our Lord.

The believer's entire armor is for his front—there is no armor for the back (no retreat)! The armor is defensive with the exception of the Sword of the Spirit (Word of God) and prayer. These two weapons are offensive.

When you have done all that you can do, just stand—and watch God work!

Scripture Reading:

Exodus 15:1-3, 6-7, 11, 18 (GNB)

> Then Moses and the Israelites sang this song to the LORD: "I will sing to the LORD, because he has won a glorious victory; he has thrown the horses and their riders into the sea. The LORD is my strong defender; he is the one who has saved me. He is my God,

and I will praise him, my father's God, and I will sing about his greatness. The LORD is a warrior; the LORD is his name.

Your right hand, LORD, is awesome in power; it breaks the enemy in pieces. In majestic triumph you overthrow your foes; your anger blazes out and burns them up like straw.

LORD, who among the gods is like you? You, LORD, will be king forever and ever."

Exodus 20:3-4 (KJV)

Thou shalt have no other gods before me. Thou shalt not make unto thee any graven image, or any likeness of any thing that is in heaven above, or that is in the earth beneath, or that is in the water under the earth: Thou shalt not bow down thyself to them, nor serve them: for I the Lord thy God am a jealous God, visiting the iniquity of the fathers upon the children unto the third and forth generation of them that hate me; And showing mercy unto thousands of them that love me, and keep my commandments.

Praise and Worship—Focal Point Readings: (KJV)

(Each Prayer Station list specific areas that concern humanity (*focal points*), and are designed to keep the prayer warrior focused while praying and interceding. Focal point scriptures are listed below so that the believer can pray according to the Word of God).

Scriptures	Focal Points
Genesis 1	Creator
Exodus 34:6-8	Mercy, gracious, long-suffering, goodness, truth, forgiving

Scriptures	Focal Points
Luke 11:2	Hallow His Name
Romans 5:10-11	Atonement

Scriptures	Focal Points
Psalm 29:4-11	Majesty
Psalm 34:1-9	Exalted
Psalm 65:6	Omnipotence
Psalm 89:14	Justice, Mercy, truth
Psalm 99:5	Holy
Psalm 113:5-6	Humble
Psalms 139:1-6	Omniscience
Psalms 139:7-11	Omnipresence
Psalms 139:12-16	Omnipotence
Jeremiah 23:5-6	Righteous, justice
Matthew 28:19	Father, Son, Holy Spirit
John 1:1-5	The Word

Scriptures	Focal Points
1 Corinthians 1:24	Wisdom
1 Corinthians 11:25	New Covenant
Colossians 1:14	Redemption
1 Thessalonians 5;24	Faithful
1 Timothy 6:15-16	Potentate, King of kings, Lord of lords
Hebrew 1:3	His Glory
Hebrew 7:14-17	Infinite
Hebrews 13:8	Immutable
1 John 4:8	Love
Revelation 1:8	Alpha, Omega
Revelation 5:11-14	Worthy

Reflections from the heart: When you reflect on what you have heard it causes you to think about how it has impacted your heart. What changes are you willing to make, or what changes have you made as a result of reflecting? Write down your reflections as you take this journey with the Lord.

Prayer Request: (Be specific!)

(Write out your petition and validate it with scriptures to ensure that it lines up with the Word of God for your life. God's Word is His will!)

Supporting Scriptures:

Date Petition Answered:

Family

Prayer Station II

*"Fear thou not; for I am with thee: be not dismayed; for
I am thy God: I will strengthen thee; yea, I will help thee;
yea, I will uphold thee with the right hand
of my righteousness."
(Isaiah 41:10 KJV)*

JESUS

Jehovah T'Sur
The Lord Our Strength
Psalm 19:14

Prayer Station II

Family

Ephesians 5:22-33
Psalm 115:14-15
Salvation
Will of God
Love—Unity
Blessings
Communication
Forgiveness
Conflict Resolution
Trust—Stability
Marriage—Singles
Widows—Single Parents
Infidelity—Divorce
Protection—Abuse
Extended Family
Aging Parents—Caregivers
Foster Care—Bereavement
Abortions—Satanic Attacks

Feet Shod with the Gospel of Peace

Prayer Station II—Family

Family is the first institution put in place by God. It is also the first creation of God that the enemy (Satan) tried to destroy by bringing disobedience to the Creator (Genesis 3). He continues his crusade to this day!

As society continues to evolve and negatively influence the family values and structure away from what God intended, prayer is the only effective weapon against this, and we have to use it.

The enemy knows that in unity there is strength. As we approach this prayer station, let us keep in mind what God intended family to be.

Jehovah T'Sur (Psalm 19:14)

Jehovah T'Sur, "the Lord our Strength"—The Psalmist realized that only the Lord could keep his soul from destruction. David prayed that the Lord would keep him from presumptuous sins and would order his conversation aright—and that his heart be found acceptable unto God who is his strength and his redeemer. Jehovah T'Sur.

"Let the words of my mouth, and the meditation of my heart, be acceptable in thy sight, O Lord, my strength, and my redeemer." (Psalm 19:14)

Family

It is appropriate to ask God to strengthen and protect the family and to keep it in His divine will. God is able to cleanse and keep the family from the corruption of this world system. The family that prays together will overcome the obstacles that come to kill, steal and destroy. Where there is unity there is strength. "He only is my rock and my salvation; he is my defense; I shall not be greatly moved" (Psalm 62:2).

The Armor

The armor for the family is that "the feet are shod with the preparation of the Gospel of Peace" (Ephesians 6:15 KJV). The feet speak of the believer's Christian walk, representing his personal conduct and character. Further it speaks of the believer's solid foundation, which is the preparation of the gospel of peace. Naturally, shoes on the feet are essential for standing, they give support and stability. So with the believer, he must be so rooted and grounded in the Word of God that he can encounter the enemy with the Word like a pen of a ready writer.

Knowing the Word of God is the groundwork (preparation) in combating against such a powerful opponent. While Jesus was in opposition with the devil in the wilderness He was prepared (preparation) to speak the weapon of the Word of God and His opponent departed for a season (Luke 4:3-4,13).

Scripture Reading:

Genesis 7:7, 15-16, 9:8, 12-17 (GNB)

> *He and his wife, and his sons and their wives, went into the boat to escape the flood. A male and a female of each kind of living being went into the boat with Noah, as God had commanded. Then the LORD shut the door behind Noah."*
>
> *God said to Noah and his sons, I am now making my covenant with you and with your descendants, . . . As a sign of this everlasting covenant, which I am making with you and with all living beings, I am putting my bow in the clouds. It will be the sign of my covenant with the world. Whenever I cover the sky with clouds and the rainbow appears, I will remember my promise to you*

and to all the animals that a flood will never again destroy all living beings. When the rainbow appears in the clouds, I will see it and remember the everlasting covenant between me and all living beings on earth. That is the sign of the promise which I am making to all living beings.

Psalm 115:14-16 (KJV)

The Lord shall increase you more and more, you and your children. Ye are blessed of the LORD, WHICH made heaven and earth. The heaven, even the heavens, are the Lord's but the earth hath he given to the children of men.

Family—Focal Point Readings: (KJV)

(Each Prayer Station list specific areas that concern humanity (*focal points*), and are designed to keep the prayer warrior focused while praying and interceding. Focal point scriptures are listed below so that the believer can pray according to the Word of God).

Scripture	Focal Point	Scripture	Focal Point
Genesis 2:18, 22-23	marriage	Matthew 6:14–15	forgiveness
Genesis 21:9-21	single parent	Matthew 19: 3-9	divorce
Genesis 22:17-18	blessings	Mark 1:29-34	extended family
Genesis 24:1-9	aging parents	John 3:15	salvation
Genesis 27:41, 33:1-4	conflict resolution	John 3:16	love
Exodus 2:9-10	foster care	John 15:13	love
Ruth 1:3-5	widows	Acts 6:1-7	widows
Job 1:12-22	bereavement	Acts 11:14	salvation
Psalm 23:4	protection	Acts 16:31	salvation
Psalm 133:1	unity	Ephesians 6:4	abuse
Psalm 139:14-16	abortions	1Corinthians 7:32-34	singles
Proverbs 3:5	trust-stability	Hebrews 13:4	infidelity
Matthew 2:13-15	satanic attacks	2 Peter 3:9	will of God

Reflections from the heart: *When* you reflect on what you have heard it causes you to think about how it has impacted your heart. What changes are you willing to make, or what changes have you made as a result of reflecting? Write down your reflection as you take this journey with the Lord.

Prayer Request: (Be specific!)

(Write out your petition and validate it with scriptures to ensure that it lines up with the Word of God for your life. God's Word is His will!)

Supporting Scriptures:

Date Petition Answered:

CHILDREN

PRAYER STATION III

"And all thy children shall be taught of the LORD; and great shall be the peace of thy children."
(Isaiah 54:13 KJV)

Jesus

Jehovah Nissi
The Lord Is My Banner
Exodus 17:15

Prayer Station III

Children

Ephesians 6:1-4
Genesis 22:17-18
Salvation
Blessed-Loved-Happy
Stability—Focus—Favor
Wisdom—Integrity
Education—Scholars
Head not the Tail
Crime—Safety—Protection
Physical—Mental Abuse
Peer Pressure—Adoption
Low Self Esteem—Teen Suicide
Rebellion—Withdrawal
Abstinence—Loneliness
Abductions
Incest—Fornication
Child Pornography—Prostitution
Homosexuality
Internet Scams

Helmet of Salvation

Prayer Station III—Children

"Behold children are a heritage from the Lord, the fruit of the womb is a reward" (Psalm 127:3 NKJV).

There has never been such an attack on children as there is today. In the home, abandonment, abortion, and abuse are all on the rise. Outside the home, abduction, slaughter, violence and distrust are some of the many dangers facing our children.

We need the Lord to protect and keep the children from the plan of the enemy to kill, steal and destroy.

Jehovah Nissi—The LORD My Banner (Exodus 17:15)

As the children of Israel fled from Egypt by way of the Sinai desert, better referred to as the "wilderness"—God began to teach them along the way to trust in the many facets of His name. The Hebrew compound name YHWH-Nissi, "the LORD is my Banner" or "the Lord is my Conquest," was demonstrated as Israel came up against opposition with Amalek in the wilderness. Amalek was the first to attack Israel as they pitched their tents at Rephidim in a desert near Mount Horeb.

Amalek did not fear God and took advantage of the Israelites as they attempted to pass through their territory. Moses instructed Joshua to choose men and go fight with Amalek, and as they fought Moses would stand on the top of the hill with the rod of God in his hand. Moses had with him Aaron and Hur. When Moses held up his hands Israel prevailed in battle, and when his hands were down Amalek prevailed. Moses became tired and he sat on a rock. Aaron and Hur held up his hands with the rod of God, one on one side and one on the other—causing Israel to be victorious in battle.

Israel won the battle against Amalek. God commanded Moses to write this for a memorial in the book, and rehearse it in the ears of

Joshua: "for I will utterly put out the remembrance of Amalek from under heaven." And Moses built an altar and called the name of it *Jehovah-Nissi*, "Because the LORD hath sworn that the LORD will have war with Amalek from generation to generation."

Jehovah-Nissi means "the LORD is my banner," or "the LORD is my sign of conquest." Moses used this name to declare that God would always conquer the enemy and meet the needs of His people. The rod in Moses' hand served as a banner demonstrating the miraculous power of God.

Children

Intercession requires others to help in the fight against sin! When interceding for children, there will be times when you will need personal prayer, corporate prayer, someone to touch and agree with you, and times when you will need heaven to bind and loose with you on their behalf.

As the believer prays and intercedes for children, the LORD will conquer every foe. Just keep your banner, (your hands) up before Him in faith, praise and worship and the LORD will bring them out of every circumstance that opposes His will for their life.

Don't allow the banner over children to be "things," the cares of this world, for "His banner over me is Love" (Song of Solomon 2:4). Communicate and listen to your children and let their concerns be your burdens in prayer.

The Armor

The armor for this prayer station is the "helmet of salvation" (Ephesians 6:17). I Thessalonians 5:8 speaks of this helmet as "the hope of salvation" or the "assurance of salvation." The believer can walk in the blessed assurance of salvation for their house.

Jesus Christ is our salvation—the helmet of salvation protects our mind, which is the battlefield of the enemy. God's appeal is to the heart and mind of man—"Let this mind be in you which was also in Christ Jesus" (Philippians 2:5). He has been made unto us salvation!

"For the weapons of our warfare are not carnal, but mighty through God to the pulling down of strongholds; casting down imaginations, and every high thing that exalteth itself against the knowledge of God, and bringing into captivity every thought to the obedience of Christ;" (2 Corinthians 10:4-6).

The way to be free of anxiety is to be prayerful with thanksgiving about everything. "Be careful for nothing; but in every thing by prayer and supplication with thanksgiving let you request be made known unto God. And the peace of God, which passeth all understanding, shall keep your heart and minds through Christ Jesus" (Philippians 4:6-7).

Scripture Reading:

Matthew 2:7, 13-18 (GNB)

> *Herod called the visitors from the East to a secret meeting and found out from them the exact time the star had appeared. Then he sent them to Bethlehem with these instructions: "Go and make a careful search for the child; and when you find him, let me know, so that I too may go and worship him." After they had left, an angel of the Lord appeared in a dream to Joseph and said, "Herod will be looking for the child in order to kill him. So get up, take the child and his mother and escape to Egypt, and stay there until I tell you to leave." Joseph got up, took the child and his mother, and left during the night for Egypt, where he stayed until Herod died. This was done to make come true what the Lord had said through the prophet, "I called my Son out of Egypt."*

When Herod realized that the visitors from the East had tricked him, he was furious. He gave orders to kill all the boys in Bethlehem and its neighborhood who were two years old and younger—this was done in accordance with what he had learned from the visitors about the time when the star had appeared.

In this way what the prophet Jeremiah had said came true: "A sound is heard in Ramah, the sound of bitter weeping, Rachel is crying for her children: she refuses to be comforted, for they are dead."

Exodus 2:9-10 (KJV)

And Pharaoh's daughter said unto her, Take this child away, and nurse it for me, and I will give thee thy wages. And the woman took the child, and nursed it. And the child grew, and she brought him unto Pharaoh's daughter, and he became her son. And she called his name Moses: and she said, Because I drew him out of the water.

Children—Focal Point Readings: (KJV)

(Each Prayer Station list specific areas that concern humanity (*focal points*), and are designed to keep the prayer warrior focused while praying and interceding. Focal point scriptures are listed below so that the believer can pray according to the Word of God).

Scripture	Focal Point
Genesis 4:1-9	crime
Genesis 19:4-14	homosexuality
Genesis 19:30-38, Leviticus 20:1-27	incest
Exodus 2:10	adoption
Deuteronomy 28:13	head not tail
1 Kings 3:5-15	wisdom
Job 1:4 – 5	protection
Psalm 1	stability
Psalm 13:1-4	loneliness
Jeremiah 20:7-9	low self esteem
Psalm 91	safety
Psalm 128:1-2	happy
Proverbs 1:7-16	peer pressure

Scripture	Focal Point
Song of Solomon 2:4	love
Daniel 1:3-9, 12:4	education
Matthew 1:23	abstinence
Mark 10-14-16	blessed
Luke 1:26-38	favor
Romans 1:26-32, 2 Timothy 3:1-9, 1 Corinthians 6: 16-20. Galatians 5:19-21	fornication, child pornography, internet scams, abductions, low self esteem, teen suicide
Romans 10:13-16	salvation
1 Corinthians 13:11	focus
2 Timothy 2:1-5	integrity

Reflections from the heart: *When* you reflect on what you have heard it causes you to think about how it has impacted your heart. What changes are you willing to make, or what changes have you made as a result of reflecting? Write down your reflections as you take this journey with the Lord.

Prayer Request: (Be specific!)

(Write out your petition and validate it with scriptures to ensure that it lines up with the Word of God for your life. God's Word is His will!)

Supporting Scriptures:

Date Petition Answered:

Finance

Prayer Station IV

"Ho, every one that thirsteth, come ye to the waters, and he that hath no money; come ye, buy, and eat; yea, come, buy wine and milk without money and without price."
(Isaiah 55:1-2 KJV)

Jesus

Jehovah Jireh
The Lord will Provide
Genesis 22:14

Prayer Station IV

Finance

Malachi 3:6-12

Wisdom—Prosperity—Wealth
Tithes—Offerings
Good Stewardship—Faithful
Give and it shall be Given
Honesty—Clean Heart
Jobs—Income—Security
Work Habits
Pledges—Debts Paid
Debts Canceled
Credit Card Debt—Taxes
Debt Free—No Lack
Investments
Stealing—Slothful—Unfaithful
Wages in Bags with Holes
Covet—Pressure
Forgiveness
Outreach—Poor

Loins Girt with Truth

Prayer Station IV—Finance

"A feast is made for laughter, and wine maketh merry, but money answereth all things" (Ecclesiastes 10:19).

In the tangible world we live in, the word of God speaks loud and clear on this truth, "Money answereth all things." At the base of much unhappiness in the world today are financial problems. It is causing strain on marriages, education, living situations, career progress, and ministry.

In a world of quick cash schemes and easily accessible credit cards, debt is becoming a cancerous burden. The enemy has been using these strategies to stop the flow of God's blessings to the believers. God is our provider; there is nothing He cannot supply. We need the Lord's provision and wisdom to overcome these challenges.

Jehovah Jireh—The LORD my Provider (Genesis 22:14)

Abraham was challenged by God to offer up his only son Isaac whom God had promised that "in Isaac shall thy seed be called" (Genesis 21:12). Abraham staggered not at the promises of God, but by faith believed that God would raise Isaac from the dead if sacrificed (Hebrews 11:17-19). However, Abraham had told the boy that God would provide a lamb for the sacrifice. His faith was great and positioned him for a blessing from God (Genesis 22:8).

Abraham's faith was tried, tested, proved and authenticated. As Abraham moved to obey God—God provided a ram for the sacrifice as spoken by Abraham. The power of life and death is in the tongue. By faith, Abraham spoke deliverance for his only son Isaac.

Isaac's faith was strong in his father, for he had the strength and the ability to come off the altar for he was a boy of over 18 years old. So, let our faith be strong in our heavenly Father who will provide for his children good things.

Abraham called the name of that place Jehovah Jireh, for "God will provide." God will provide a ram for the sacrifice—all you have to do is offer it back to him willing.

God's work done according to His will cannot fail to have His provisions. He is a God who sees your needs and provides for them.

Let us be good stewards of what God has entrusted us with. Be obedient to the requirements of giving, for it was God who provided the ultimate sacrifice when He offered up His only begotten Son to die for the sins of the entire world. Obedience is better than sacrifice and is the key to power with God.

Finance

God blessed Abraham with wealth before He blessed him with spiritual Isaac. It is the Fathers desire to give you the kingdom. Pray to God the Father in the name of Jesus that He will heal your finances. Ask Him to teach you how to manage and be a good steward over what he has entrusted into your hands. Ask God to teach you how to give in tithes, offerings and how to consider the poor.

"Speak unto the children of Israel, that they bring me an offering: of every man that giveth it willingly with his heart ye shall take my offering" (Exodus 25:2).

"Thou hast bought me no sweet cane with money, neither hast thou filled me with the fat of thy sacrifices:" (Isaiah 43:24a)

"Blessed is he that considereth the poor: the LORD will deliver him in time of trouble" (Psalm 41:1).

The Armor

The armor for this station is the "loins gird with truth" (Ephesians 6:14). Our spiritual belt for the loins is the Word of God, which is the central hub that holds the other pieces of the armor in place. "Truth" is the knowledge of the *truth* of God's Word.

The loins are our reproductive system, where we bring forth life (birth). Therefore, it is essential that our loins are gird about with *truth* so that we will bring forth those things that are righteous and bring glory to the Father. God's word is truth.

"Out of your belly shall flow rivers of living water" (John 7:38).

Scripture Reading:

Deuteronomy 14:22-26 (KJV)

> *Thou shalt truly tithe all the increase of thy seed, that the field bringeth forth year by year. And thou shalt eat before the LORD thy God, in the place he shall choose to place his name there, the tithe of thy corn, of thy wine, and of thine oil, and the firstlings of thy herds and of thy flocks; that thou mayest learn to fear the LORD thy God always. And if the way be too long for thee, so that thou art not able to carry it; or if the place be too far from thee, which the LORD thy God shall choose to set his name there, when the LORD thy God hath blessed thee:*

> *Then shalt thou turn it into money, and bind up the money in thine hand, and shalt go unto the place which the LORD thy God shall choose: And thou shalt bestow that money for whatsoever thy soul lusteth after, for oxen, or for sheep, or for wine, or for strong drink, or for whatsoever thy soul desireth: and thou shalt eat there before the LORD thy God, and shalt rejoice, thou, and thine household.*

Malachi 3:10-11 (KJV)

> *Bring ye all the tithes into the storehouse, that there may be meat in mine house, and prove me now herewith, saith the LORD of*

hosts, if I will not open you the windows of heaven, and pour you out a blessing, that there shall not be room enough to receive it. And I will rebuke the devourer for your sakes, and he shall not destroy the fruits of your ground; neither shall your vine cast her fruit before the time in the field, saith the LORD *of hosts.*

Finance—Focal Point Readings: (KJV)

(Each Prayer Station list specific areas that concern humanity (*focal points*), and are designed to keep the prayer warrior focused while praying and interceding. Focal point scriptures are listed below so that the believer can pray according to the Word of God).

Scripture	Focal Point	Scripture	Focal Point
Exodus 30-11-16	pledges	Luke 6: 38-44	give-given
Deuteronomy 16:17, Deuteronomy 14:22-29	offerings, tithings	Luke 7:41-43	forgiveness
Psalm 49:6-8, 62:10-11	prosperity	Luke 12:13-17	covet
Psalm 51:10	clean heart	Luke 12:22-30	pressure
Psalm 66:12	wealthy	Luke 12:41-48	unfaithful
Proverbs 13:22	security	Luke 16:1-12	stewardship
Proverbs 18:9, 21:25	slothful	Revelations 3:7-13	faithful
Proverbs 19:17	outreach, poor	Luke 19:12-27	investments
Proverbs 23:4-5	wisdom	Acts 5:1-11	stealing
Isaiah 55:1-3	security	Deuteronomy 15:1-18	debt free
Haggai 1:3 –12	tithes, offerings	Romans 13:7	taxes
Malachi 3:6-12	tithes, offerings	1 Thessalonians 4:11	work habits
Matthew 20:1-8	work habits	1 Thessalonians 4:12	honesty, no lack

Reflections from the heart: When you reflect on what you have heard it causes you to think about how it has impacted your heart. What changes are you willing to make, or what changes have you made as a result of reflecting? Write down your reflections as you take this journey with the Lord.

Prayer Request: (Be specific!)

(Write out your petition and validate it with scriptures to ensure that it lines up with the Word of God for your life. God's Word is His will!)

Supporting Scriptures:

Date Petition Answered:

Healing

Prayer Station V

"Therefore will I divide him a portion with the great, and he shall divide the spoil with the strong; because he hath poured out his soul unto death: and he was numbered with the transgressors; and he bare the sin of many, and made intercession for the transgressors."
(Isaiah 53:12 KJV)

JESUS

Jehovah Rophe
The Lord Who Heals
Exodus 15:26

Prayer Station V

Healing

Isaiah 53, I Peter 2:24-25
Miracles—Signs—Wonders
Mental—Physical—Spiritual
Spirit of Infirmity
Diseases
High Blood Pressure
AIDS
Cancer—Diabetes
Heart—Kidney Disease
Tumors—Arteries
Disorders
Arthritis
Depression
Headaches—Attention Deficit
Gum Disease
Reproductive Failure
Anger—Fear
Grief—Trauma

Shield of Faith

Prayer Station V—Healing

A growing number of sicknesses and disease afflict the world today. Doctors and psychologists are overwhelmed. Sin is the spiritual sickness that plagues the world.

The physical healing God provides is symbolic of the spiritual restoration He longs for with His people. He spoke to Solomon, "If My people who are called by My name will humble themselves, and pray and seek my face, and turn from their wicked ways, then I will hear from heaven, and will forgive their sin and heal their land" (II Chronicles 7:14 NKJV).

As God says in Exodus, He is "the Lord that healeth." Jesus was sent as the final remedy to all sin, sickness, and disease, both spiritual and physical. Each miracle performed by Jesus in the New Testament was an example of the healing that He is to the world.

That same healing and restoration power is available today as you visit each prayer station.

Jehovah Rophe—The LORD who heals (Exodus 15:26)

Jehovah Rophe means "the God who heals and makes whole." The word "rophe" means to heal, to cure, and to restore. This powerful name of God is used for the first time in Exodus 15:26, where God healed the bitter waters of Marah. Jehovah Rophe heals the physical, mental and spiritual parts of man—body, soul and spirit.

When Israel was dying in the wilderness from snakebites because of their sin. Moses prayed to God for the deliverance of the people. God commanded him to make a fiery serpent of brass (symbolic of Jesus Christ the healer) and put it on a pole and whosoever look upon the serpent on the pole would live (Numbers 21:8-9). Those who were obedient looked and were healed.

"And as Moses lifted up the serpent in the wilderness, even so must the Son of man be lifted. That whosoever believeth in him should not perish, but have eternal life" (John 3:14-15).

Healing

Obedience is an important component to being healed and keeping your hearing. The LORD can make your bitter experiences sweet. Not only does He heal, but He restores all that is affected by your bitter experience. "Beloved, I wish above all things that thou mayest prosper and be in health, even as thy soul prospereth" (3 John 2). The LORD wants His children to be whole. Pray for total obedience to the Word and will of God and believe Him by faith for your healing.

"Who his own self bare our sins in his own body on the tree, that we, being dead to sins, should live unto righteousness: by whose stripes ye were healed" (1Peter 2:24).

The Armor

The armor for this station is the "shield of faith" wherewith ye shall be able to quench all the fiery darts of the wicked (Ephesians 6:16). The shield of faith is taking God at His word by believing what the Word says about Him and believing His promises. Hold your shield up to protect your mind, heart, loins and your feet. There is no armor for your back, therefore, there is no retreat!

The shield of faith protects from the fiery darts of the wicked. Satan's fiery darts afflicts our bodies from top to bottom. The fiery dart of cancer, aids, depression, grief, anger, arthritis, heart, lung and kidney disease, just to name a few. However, there is a name (JESUS) that is *above every name* and higher than the name; cancer, aids, depression, grief, anger, arthritis, heart, hung and kidney disease.

The name of Jesus is *above every name* that comes up against you. Use your spiritual authority and stand against the wiles and strategies of the devil. You have the power of attorney to use the name of JESUS! "In my name ye shall cast out devils;" . . . (Mark 16:17b). The name of JESUS is above every name—and yours for the using!

"No weapon formed against you shall prosper; and every tongue that shall rise against thee in judgment thou shalt condemn. This is the heritage of the servants of the Lord, and their righteousness is of me, saith the Lord" (Isaiah 54:17).

Scripture Reading:

Isaiah 53:4-10 (GNB)

> *But he endured the suffering that should have been ours, the pain that we should have borne. All the while we thought that his suffering was punishment sent by God. But because of our sins he was wounded, beaten because of the evil we did. We are healed by the punishment he suffered, made whole by the blows he received. All of us were like sheep that were lost, each of us going his own way. But the LORD made the punishment fall on him, the punishment all of us deserved.*
>
> *He was treated harshly, but endured it humbly; he never said a word. Like a lamb about to be slaughtered, like a sheep about to be sheared, he never said a word. He was arrested and sentenced and led off to die, and no one cared about his fate. He was put to death for the sins of our people. He was placed in a grave with those who are evil, he was buried with the rich, even though he had never committed a crime or ever told a lie."*
>
> *The LORD says, "it was my will that he should suffer; his death was a sacrifice to bring forgiveness. And so he will see his descendants; he will live a long life, and through him my purpose will succeed."*

Healing—Focal Point Readings: (KJV)

(Each Prayer Station list specific areas that concern humanity (*focal points*), and are designed to keep the prayer warrior focused while praying and interceding. Focal point scriptures are listed below so that the believer can pray according to the Word of God).

Scripture	Focal Point	Scripture	Focal Point
Genesis 17:15-19, 21-2	reproductive failure	Jeremiah 15:15-18	Grief, mental
Deuteronomy 28:15-68	disobedience, curse, diseases	Jeremiah 20:7-18	depression
Deuteronomy 28:27	tumors	Matthew 4:23	diseases
Deuteronomy 28:28,33	disorders, mental, depression, attention deficit	Matthew 9:20-22	disease
Deuteronomy 28: 34-35	anger, arthritis	Acts 4:30, 5:12	miracles, signs, wonders
Deuteronomy 28:59-61	AIDS	Romans 15:1	infirmity
2 Kings 4:19-37	headaches	Jeremiah 20:7-13	depression
Psalms 91:9-12		Colossians 3:8	anger
Isaiah 61:1-4	grief, trauma	3 John 2	mental, physical
2 Kings 20:1-11	tumors	Revelation 22:2-3	mental, physical, spiritual

Reflections from the heart: When you reflect on what you have heard, it causes you to think about how it has impacted your heart. What changes are you willing to make, or what changes have you made as a result of reflecting? Write down your reflections as you take this journey with the Lord.

Prayer Request: (Be specific!)

(Write out your petition and validate it with scriptures to ensure that it lines up with the Word of God for your life. God's Word is His will!)

Supporting Scriptures:

Date Petition Answered:

BINDING SATAN

PRAYER STATION VI

"No weapon that is formed against thee shall prosper; and every tongue that shall rise against thee in judgement thou shall condemn. This is the heritage of the servants of the LORD, and their righteousness is of me, saith the LORD."
(Isaiah 54:17 KJV)

JESUS

El Gibor
The Mighty God
Isaiah 9:6, 10:21

Prayer Station VI

Binding Satan

I John 3:8
Matthew 12:22-32

Mind is the Battlefield
Schemes of the Devil
Cancel His Assignments
Resist Him
Liar—Murderer—Thief
Deceiver-Accuser-Slander
Malice—Hatred
As a Roaring Lion
Atmosphere—Domain
Principalities—Powers
Rulers of Darkness
Spiritual Wickedness
Witchcraft—Disobedience
Unforgiveness
Unbelief—Discord—Blasphemy
Pride—Coveting
Hands that Shed Innocent Blood

The Sword of the Spirit—Word of God

Prayer Station VI—Binding Satan

"Or else how can one enter into a strong man's house, and spoil his goods, except he first bind the strong man? And then he will spoil his house" (Matthew 12:29).

Satan despises the people of God and desires to ruin God's plan of eternal life for all. He also knows that the blessings of God belong with God's people. Satan's plan is to deceive and discourage God's people. He does not want to see us blessed, and especially does not want us to make it to heaven, but rather to join him in hell. We have hope in the truth that Jesus came to destroy the works of the devil (I John 3:8).

We must be as persistent to bind Satan in Jesus' name, as he is to attack, hinder, and deceive us.

El Gibor—The Mighty God (Isaiah 9:6)

El Gibor the Mighty God is the strongest of the titles in Isaiah 9:6. "El" is always used of God and *never* refers to man. Gibor means "Hero". Together "El" and "Gibor" describes God Himself as "the hero." The child in this passage is the same divine Child as Immanuel. Speaking in the prophetic perfect, the prophet sees Him as if he is already born (Nelson study bible, p1031).

El Gibor is the perfect name for this station—for it will take the sinless blood of Jesus Christ to destroy the works of the devil. For He (Jesus) is the seed that will deliver the deathblow that will crush the head of the serpent. (Genesis 3:15).

An individual's actions will conform to the character of his true father, either God or Satan. The person born of God will reflect a Christ like behavior.

"He that committeth sin is of the devil; for the devil sinneth from the beginning. For this purpose the Son of God was manifested, that he might destroy the works of the devil" (1 John 3:8).

Binding Satan

As believers we have the authority to use the name of Jesus. In His name we shall "cast out devils, speak with new tongues, take up serpents, and if we drink any deadly thing it shall not hurt us, we shall lay hand on the sick and they shall recover" (Mark 16:17-18). No weapon formed against us shall prosper and we are more than conquers through Jesus Christ who died and gave Himself for us. Use your power to resist, bind and destroy the works of the devil.

Remember, if you do not obey God—Satan and his imps (small demons) will not obey you. The key to binding Satan is obedience to God, and the Word is God.

The Armor

The armor for this station is the Sword of the Spirit, which is the Word of God (Ephesians 6:17). It is the Word of God upon an obedient life that destroys the works of the devil. In the wilderness of temptation—Jesus used the Word of God on Satan and he left His presence for a season. The Word of God is a powerful weapon in this war against sin.

The Sword of the Spirit is the first offensive weapon mentioned in this arsenal of weapons and is one of two. The Word of God is a supernatural, offensive and powerful weapon against the enemy. Also, when you praise God through the word it paralyzes the enemy and sets him in derision.

"For the word of God is quick, and powerful, and sharper than any two-edged sword, piercing even to the dividing asunder of soul and spirit, and of the joints and marrow, and is a discerner of the thoughts and intents of the heart" (Hebrew 4:12).

"And they overcame him (Satan) by the blood of the Lamb, and by the word of their testimony;" (Revelation 12:11a). Use your Sword of the Spirit, which is the Word of God, and destroy the works of the Devil.

Scripture Reading:

Matthew 12:22-32 (GNB)

> *Then some people brought to Jesus a man who was blind and could not talk because he had a demon. Jesus healed the man, so that he was able to talk and see. The crowds were all amazed at what Jesus had done. "Could he be the Son of David?" they asked. When the Pharisees heard this, they replied, "He drives out demons only because their ruler Beelzebub gives him power to do so.*
>
> *Jesus knew what they were thinking, and so he said to them, "Any country that divides itself into groups which fight each other will not last very long. Any town or family that divides itself into groups which fight each other will fall apart. So if one group is fighting another in Satan's kingdom, this means that it is already divided into groups and will soon fall apart!*
>
> *You say that I drive out demons because Beelzebub gives me the power to do so. Well, then, who gives your followers the power to drive them out? What your own followers do proves that you are wrong! No, it is not Beelzebub, but God's Spirit, who gives me the power to drive out demons, which proves that the Kingdom of God has already come upon you.*
>
> *No one can break into a strong man's house and take away his belongings unless he first ties up the strong man; then he can plunder his house. Anyone who is not for me is really against me;*

anyone who does not help me gather is really scattering. For this reason I tell you: people can be forgiven any sin and any evil thing they say; but whoever says evil things against the Holy Spirit will not be forgiven.

Binding Satan—Focal Point Readings: (KJV)

(Each Prayer Station list specific areas that concern humanity (*focal points*), and are designed to keep the prayer warrior focused while praying and interceding. Focal point scriptures are listed below so that the believer can pray according to the Word of God).

Scripture	Focal Point	Scripture	Focal Point
Exodus 22:18	witchcraft	2 Corinthians 2:11	schemes/devil
1 Samuel 15:23	disobedience	2 Corinthians 10:3-6	mind battlefield
Proverbs 6:16-19	innocent blood, pride, wickedness, liar, discord	Ephesians 2:2	atmosphere, domain
Proverbs 8:13	pride	Ephesians 5:3	coveting
Matthew 16:18-19 Luke 10:17-18	cancel assignment	Ephesians 6:10-20 Romans 8:38-39	principalities, powers, rulers, wickedness
Mark 11:25-26	unforgiveness	1 Timothy 1:20	blasphemy
Luke 6:37, 17:3	forgiveness	James 4:7	resist
John 8:44, 10:10	liar, murderer	1 Peter 5:8-11	as a roaring lion
1 Corinthians 5:8	malice, wickedness	Jude 9	accuser, slander

Reflections from the heart: When you reflect on what you have heard it causes you to think about how it has impacted your heart. What changes are you willing to make, or what changes have you made as a result of reflecting? Write down your reflections as you take this journey with the Lord.

Prayer Request: (Be specific!)

(Write out your petition and validate it with scriptures to ensure that it lines up with the Word of God for your life. God's Word is His will!)

Supporting Scriptures:

Date Petition Answered:

LEADERSHIP

PRAYER STATION VII

"Behold, they shall surely gather together, but not by me: whosoever shall gather together against thee shall fall for thy sake."
(Isaiah 54:15 KJV)

JESUS

Jehovah Tsidkenu
The Lord our Righteousness
Jeremiah 23:6

Prayer Station VII

Leadership

Romans 13
Family
Churches
Pastor—Spouse
Pastors—Elders—Ministers
Church Leadership
Five Fold Ministry
Laborers for the Harvest
Peace of Jerusalem
Authorities
Neighborhood Watch
County—City—State Government
National Government
President of USA
Nations
Police—Fire Department
Armed Forces
Homeland Security
Employers—Educators
Schools—Colleges—Universities

Breast Plate of Righteousness

Prayer Station VII—Leadership

In today's climate of growing ministries, developing communities, and international conflicts, our religious, educational, and governmental leadership needs the wisdom and guidance of God. Whether we acknowledge it or not, the decisions our local, state, and national government makes affect the people. Sadly, many people in leadership either don't have the relationship, or take the time to seek guidance from God. Without God, man is left to himself.

We need people of integrity, justice, and wisdom in leadership today.

Jehovah Tsidkenu—The LORD our Righteousness (Jeremiah 23:6)

Jehovah Tsidkenu means "the LORD our Righteousness." The word "tsidkenu" means straightness, righteous, justice and truth. The essential meaning is unswerving adherence to the standard of fairness. Tsidkenu is also closely associated with peace in Psalm 85:10b, "Righteousness and peace have kissed each other." (The Hebrew-Greek Key Word Study Bible, p1662)

Jehovah Tsidkenu is the name that God will use to hail Christ at His Second Coming, when He returns for the salvation and safety of His people. God has imputed His righteousness to us through Christ Jesus His Son, a standing that the believer could never achieve on his own. For God Himself is the sovereign and righteous judge of the universe.

Leadership

We are to pray and intercede for all leadership, both spiritual and secular (1 Timothy 2:1-8). It is God who puts leaders into place for our protection. His desire is that they be righteous. "Offer the sacrifices of righteousness, and put your trust in the LORD" (Psalm 4:5, KJV). The righteousness that God requires must be provided by Him, for the word of God declares that we are the righteousness of God in Christ Jesus!

The Armor

The armor for this station is the "breast plate of righteous" or "the breastplate which is righteousness" (Ephesians 6:14). Jesus Christ is the righteousness of the believer. He is the rock of our salvation. This righteousness represents Christ like character and moral conduct. Obedience to the truth of God's word produces a holy life.

"If I regard iniquity in my heart then the LORD will not hear me" (Psalms 66:18). Our prayers need to come from a clean repentant heart. "Keep your heart with all diligence for out of it are the issues of life" (Proverbs 4:23).

Scripture Reading:

Romans 13:1-7 (GNB)

> Everyone must obey state authorities, because no authority exists without God's permission, and the existing authorities have been put there by God. Whoever opposes the existing authority opposes what God has ordered; and anyone who does so will bring judgment on himself. For rulers are not to be feared by those who do good, but by those who do evil. Would you like to be unafraid of those in authority? Then do what is good, and they will praise you, because they are God's servants working for your own good. But if you do evil, then be afraid of them, because their power to punish is real. They are God's servants and carry out God's punishment on those who do evil. For this reason you must obey the authorities—not just because of God's punishment, but also as

a matter of conscience. That is also why you pay taxes, because the authorities are working for God when they fulfill their duties. Pay, then, what you owe them; pay them your personal and property taxes, and show respect and honor for them all.

I Timothy 2:1-8 (KJV)

I exhort therefore, that, first of all, supplications, prayers, intercessions, and giving of thanks, be made for all men; For kings, and for all that are in authority; that we may lead a quiet and peaceable life in all godliness and honesty. For this is good and acceptable in the sight of God our Savior; who will have all men to be saved, and to come unto the knowledge of the truth. For there is one God, and one mediator between God and men, the man Christ Jesus; Who gave himself a ransom for all, to be testified in due time.

Leadership—Focal Point Readings: (KJV)

(Each Prayer Station list specific areas that concern humanity (*focal points*), and are designed to keep the prayer warrior focused while praying and interceding. Focal point scriptures are listed below so that the believer can pray according to the Word of God).

Scripture	Focal Point	Scripture	Focal Point
Judges 4:1-8	pastor-spouse	Luke 10:2	laborers for harvest
1 Samuel 3:1-9	church leadership	Luke 10:25-37	neighborhood watch
1 Samuel 15:10-23	leadership	Acts 5:33-40	educators, universities
Psalm 8:4-9		Romans 14:9-23	
Psalm 122:6	peace of Jerusalem	Ephesians 4:11 5	five fold ministry
Proverbs 14:34	nations	Ephesians 5:22-33	pastor-spouse
Proverbs 16:12	President	Ephesians 6:5-9	authorities
Proverbs 29:4	government	1 Timothy 3:1-13	church leadership, pastors, elders
Daniel 2:46-49	leadership	1 Timothy 5:17-18	elders
Amos 3:1-8	family	1 Timothy 6:15-16	
Matthew 16:18, Revelations 3:7-13	church	Hebrews 12:14	
Mark 12:13-17	county, city, state, national government	Hebrews 13:17, Titus 3:1-2	authorities, leadership
Romans 13:1-7, 1 Timothy 2:1-8	armed forces, police		

Reflections from the heart: When you reflect on what you have heard it causes you to think about how it has impacted your heart. What changes are you willing to make, or what changes have you made as a result of reflecting? Write down your reflections as you take this journey with the Lord.

Prayer Request: (Be specific!)

(Write out your petition and validate it with scriptures to ensure that it lines up with the Word of God for your life. God's Word is His will!)

Supporting Scriptures:

Date Petition Answered:

UNITY

PRAYER STATION VIII

"For thus saith the high and lofty One that inhabiteth eternity, whose name is Holy; I dwell in the high and holy place, with him also that is of a contrite and humble spirit, to revive the spirit of the humble, and to revive the heart of the contrite ones."
(Isaiah 57:15 KJV)

JESUS

Immanuel
God with Us
Matthew 1:23

Prayer Station VIII

Unity

John 17

Love of God
Body of Christ
One Body—Many Members
Oneness
That The World May Believe
Mind of Christ
Corporate in Prayer
Prayer of Agreement
Christ Glorified in Us
Cleanse—Sanctify Us
Focused—None be Lost
Bearing One Another
Long Suffering
Unity of the Spirit—Faith
Divisions—Rebellion
Binding and Loosing

Praying always with all prayer in the Spirit

Prayer Station VIII—Unity

Division is one of the biggest enemies of humanity. The enemy knows that when the people are one, nothing they propose to do will be withheld from them (Genesis 11:6).

The disciples were filled with the Holy Spirit on the day of Pentecost when they were on "one accord" (Acts 2:1-4). Unity is especially necessary in the church and the family; moreover, it is God's desire for his people to be one as He and Christ are one (John 11:17).

Immanuel—God with Us (Matthew 1:23)

Immanuel means "God with Us." It speaks of the incarnate Son of God who is pictured in Isaiah 9:6-7 as the Child Prince. "For unto us a child is born, ... the Prince of Peace." The name Immanuel is often identified with the virgin birth of Christ (Isaiah 7:14, Matthew 1:23).

Immanuel is a title describing the deity of the person of the Son of God rather than a name actually used by Him. It implies that God will come to dwell among His people in the person of Jesus Christ the God-man (Nelson's study bible p1405).

Jesus prays, for those whom the Father has given him and for those who believe in Him through their word. That they all may be one; as He and the Father are one that the world may believe that God has sent Him. He has also given believers the glory that the Father has given him that they may be made perfect in one. And the Father has loved them as He has loved His Son (John 17:21).

Unity

The virgin birth of Immanuel allows the perfect sacrifice for He was born without sin. If you look at the word atonement you will find "at-one-ment." The believer is "at-one" with the Father (unity) though the death, burial, and resurrection of Jesus Christ. Immanuel allows the believer to come into the presence of the Almighty God.

All this speaks of unity—there is power in unity (oneness). Unity is preciousness and blessedness. Prayer brings about unity.

Unity of the believer includes:

1. binding and loosing (Matthew 16:19)
2. one accord in one place (Acts 2:1)
3. corporate prayer (Acts 4:31)
4. prayer of agreement (any two touching and agreeing Matthew 18:19)
5. allow the Holy Spirit to make intercession according to the will of God (Romans 8:26)

The Armor

The armor for this station is "Praying always with all prayer and supplication in the Spirit" (Ephesians 6:18a). Without prayer the armor is inadequate. The believer is to lay hold of God for spiritual resources. Praying always means on every occasion, even before the enemy attacks.

At this station the believer is asked to do something as a result of having on the whole armor—they are to pray. "Praying always with all prayer and supplication in the Spirit, and watching thereunto with all perseverance and supplication for all saints" (Ephesians 6:18). Prayer is indispensable and powerful.

Praying in the Spirit—the Spirit has divine insight and prays classified information—which is the will of God. Prayer is unity with God.

"Likewise the Spirit also helpeth our infirmities: for we know not what we should pray for as we ought: but the Spirit itself maketh intercession for us with groanings which cannot be uttered. And he that searcheth the hearts knoweth what is the mind of the Spirit, because he maketh intercession for the saints according to the will of God" (Romans 8:26).

Scripture Reading:

John 17:6-11, 20-26 (GNB)

> *I have made you known to those you gave me out of the world. They belonged to you, and you gave them to me. They have obeyed your word, and now they know that everything you gave me comes from you. I gave them the message that you gave me, and they received it; they know that it is true that I came from you, and they believe that you sent me. I pray for them, I do not pray for the world but for those you gave me, for they belong to you.*
>
> *All I have is yours, and all you have is mine; and my glory is shown through them. And now I am coming to you; I am no longer in the world, but they are in the world. Holy Father! Keep them safe by the power of your name, the name you gave me, so that they may be one just as you and I are one.*
>
> *I pray not only for them, but also for those who believe in me because of their message. I pray that they may all be one. Father! May they be in us, just as you are in me and I am in you. May they be one, so that the world will believe that you sent me. I gave them the same glory you gave me, so that they may be completely one, just as you and I are one.*
>
> *I in them and you in me, so that they may be completely one, in order that the world may know that you sent me and that you love them as you love me.*

1 Thessalonians 5:16-24 (KJV)

Rejoice evermore. Pray without ceasing. In everything give thanks: for this is the will of God in Christ Jesus concerning you. Quench not the Spirit. Despise not prophesying. Prove all things; hold fast that which is good. Abstain from all appearance of evil. And the very God of peace sanctify you wholly; and I pray God your whole spirit and soul and body be preserved blameless unto the coming of our Lord Jesus Christ. Faithful is he that calleth you, who also will do it.

Unity—Focal Point Readings: (KJV)

(Each Prayer Station list specific areas that concern humanity (*focal points*), and are designed to keep the prayer warrior focused while praying and interceding. Focal point scriptures are listed below so that the believer can pray according to the Word of God).

Scripture	Focal Point	Scripture	Focal Point
Genesis 11:1-6	oneness, focused	1 Corinthians 12:14-26	one body, many members
Psalm 51:2-4	cleanse, sanctify us	1 Corinthians 6:19-20	
Psalm 133	spirit of unity	Galatians 5:22-26	long suffering
Matthew 16:19	binding loosing	Ephesians 4:3-6	one body, unit of the Spirit, faith
Matthew 18:19	prayer of agreement	Galatians 6:1-5	
John 17	world may believe, none be lost, Christ glorified in us, sanctify	Philippians 2:5	focused, mind of Christ
Acts 2:42	corporate prayer	Hebrews 2:11	sanctify us
Romans 5:1-5	love of God	James 5:13-16	corporate prayer
Romans 12:1-2	mind of Christ	1 John 1:5-7	cleanse us
Romans 15:1-6	bearing one another		
Romans 16:17	divisions, rebellion		

Reflections from the heart: When you reflect on what you have heard it causes you to think about how it has impacted your heart. What changes are you willing to make, or what changes have you made as a result of reflecting? Write down your reflections as you take this journey with the Lord.

Prayer Request: (Be specific!)

(Write out your petition and validate it with scriptures to ensure that it lines up with the Word of God for your life. God's Word is His will!)

Supporting Scriptures:

Date Petition Answered:

PRISONERS/CAPTIVES

PRAYER STATION IX

"To appoint unto them that mourn in Zion, to give unto them beauty for ashes, the oil of joy for mourning, the garment of praise for the spirit of heaviness; that they might be called trees of righteousness, the planting of the LORD, that he might be glorified."
(Isaiah 61:3 KJV)

JESUS

Jehovah Shammah
The Lord is There
Ezekiel 48:35

Prayer Station IX

Prisoners—Captives

Luke 4:18-19

Salvation—Depravity—Sin
Freedom—Protection
Deliverance from Satan
Undo Burdens—Chains—Fetters
Spirit of Fear—Suicide
Possessed—Oppressive Spirits
Preach the Gospel
Open Prison Doors
Heal the Broken Hearted
Sight to the Blind
Free the Bruised
Dumb Speak—Lame Walk
Wickedness
Oil of Joy for Mourning
Garment of Praise for Heaviness
The Anointing Destroys Yokes

Watching with all Perseverance for all Saints

Prayer Station IX—Prisoners / Captives

Prisons worldwide are filled to capacity and steadily growing. In addition, there are those in mental captivity caused by physical limitations, fear, and the strategies of Satan. Many entangled by these strongholds have both given up on themselves and have been forgotten by the outside world and the household of faith. However, one of the prophesied missions of Jesus was, "to set at liberty those who are oppressed" (Luke 4:18-19).

Through intercession, we give hope to those who are oppressed by the devil.

Jehovah Shammah—The Lord is There (Ezekiel 48:35)

Jehovah Shammah means, "the LORD is there." In Ezekiel 48:35, God promises the Israelites who were captive in Babylon that he would restore His presence in Jerusalem. The LORD Himself will be there and the name of the city would be "The Lord is there." There would be twelve gates to the city named after the twelve tribes of Israel. This prophecy of hope lets Israel know that Jerusalem would be restored. God tells Ezekiel that the name of the New Jerusalem would be Jehovah Shammah, "the LORD is there."

Captives/Prisoners

No matter what your plight may be, God is there. He has promised that he will never leave you nor forsake you. The LORD is always there. In the nursing homes, sick and shut in, hospitals, behind prison doors or captive in your mind—the LORD is there. Jesus came to set the captives free. "The Word became flesh and dwelt among us and we beheld His glory" (John 1:14).

The Armor

The armor for this station is "watching thereunto with all

perseverance and supplication for all saints" (Ephesians 6:18b). This means being guarded and unmovable in your prayer life on every occasion and for all the saints. Supplication is prayer for certain benefits (Luke 1:13, 1 Timothy 2:1). In the Greek it is *"deesis"* meaning a request for specific benefits from God or anyone else.

Pray for yourself, family, the saints, leadership and the unbelievers. Ask for the benefits, promises of God's Word. Watching is praying, perseverance, supplications and standing guard for those entrusted in your spiritual care. It is not God's will that any man should perish. Spiritual warfare is for individual and corporate conflict. "Watch and pray, that ye enter not into temptation, the spirit indeed is willing, but the flesh is weak" (Matthew 26:41).

Pray God's word always. Put the holy word of God up against Satan's slander—because he (Satan) is a liar and cannot tell the truth.

Scripture Reading:

Acts 12:5-9, 16 (GNB)

> *So Peter was kept in jail, but the people of the church were praying earnestly to God for him.*
>
> *The night before Herod was going to bring him out to the people, Peter was sleeping between two guards. He was tied with two chains, and there were guards on duty at the prison gate. Suddenly and angel of the Lord stood there, and a light shone in the cell. The angel shook Peter by the shoulder, woke him up, and said, "Hurry! Get up!" At once the chains fell off Peter's hands. Then the angel said, "Tighten your belt and put on your sandals." Peter did so, and the angel said, "Put your cloak around you and come with me." Peter followed him out of the prison, not knowing, however, if what the angel was doing was real; he thought he was*

seeing a vision. They passed by the first guard station and then the second, and came at last to the iron gate that opens into the city. The gate opened for them by itself, and walked down a street, and suddenly the angel left Peter.

Meanwhile Peter kept on knocking. At last they opened the door, and when they saw him, they were amazed.

Luke 4:18-19 (KJV)

The Spirit of the LORD is upon me, because he hath anointed me to preach the gospel to the poor; he hath sent me to heal the brokenhearted, to preach deliverance to the captives, and recovering of sight to the blind, to set at liberty them that are bruised, to preach the acceptable year of the LORD.

Prisoners / Captives—Focal Point Readings: (KJV)

(Each Prayer Station list specific areas that concern humanity (*focal points*), and are designed to keep the prayer warrior focused while praying and interceding. Focal point scriptures are listed below so that the believer can pray according to the Word of God).

Scripture	Focal Point	Scripture	Focal Point
Psalm 119:134	oppression	Luke 4:18	preach the gospel, heal broken hearted, blind, free bruised
Proverbs 8:7	wickedness	Acts 5:16, 12:7-8, 16:25-28	
Isaiah 10:27	anointing breaks yokes	Acts 16:16-18	possessed
Isaiah 35:3-6	deliverance	Romans 10:13-16	salvation
Isaiah 61:1-3	broken heart, prison doors, oil of joy for mourning, spirit of praise for heaviness	Hebrew 12:1-4 Hebrews 12:12-14	depravity-sin freedom
Matthew 27:3-6	suicide	Hebrews 13:3	undo burdens
Mark 5:1-20	deliverance from Satan, demon possessed	1 Peter 5:7-8	protection
Mark 5:2-19	burdens, chains, fetters	1 John 2:12-14	depravity-sin
Mark 9:23-29	dumb speak, freedom	1 John 4:18	spirit of fear

Reflections from the heart: When you reflect on what you have heard it causes you to think about how it has impacted your heart. What changes are you willing to make, or what changes have you made as a result of reflecting? Write down your reflections as you take this journey with the Lord.

Prayer Request: (Be specific!)
(Write out your petition and validate it with scriptures to ensure that it lines up with the Word of God for your life. God's Word is His will!)

Supporting Scriptures:

Date Petition Answered:

BONDAGE

PRAYER STATION X

"Thus saith thy Lord the Lord, and thy God that pleadeth the cause of his people, Behold, I have taken out of thine hand the cup of trembling, even the dregs of the cup of my fury; thou shall no more drink it again: But I will put it into the hand of them that afflict thee; which have said to thy soul, Bow down, that we may go over: and thou hast laid thy body as the ground, and as the street, to them that went over."
(Isaiah 51:22-23 KJV)

JESUS

Jehovah Shalom
The Lord is Peace
Judges 6:24

Prayer Station X

Bondage

John 8:33-36
Love of God
Sin
Depression—Oppression
Illusions
Insecurity
Confusion—Fear
Abuse—Rejection
Homeless
Unforgiveness
Emotional Pain—Affliction
Low Self Esteem
Egoism—Conflict
Illiterate—Reactive
Unequally Yoked
Relationships—Cultural
Childhood Bondage
Generational Curses

Having Done All to Stand

Prayer Station X—Bondage

Bondage is one of the enemy's most effective tactics against God's people. Individuals being controlled by anxieties such as: childhood experiences, troubled marriages, mental abuse, divorce, alcohol, drugs, and pornography, among many others, are in bondage.

Only those whom Jesus sets free is free indeed (John 8:36). We need God to loose the captive and set them free through His divine weapon of intercession.

Jehovah Shalom—The Lord is Peace (Judges 6:24)

When you worship and praise God in the midst of trouble He will reveal precious and powerful things about Himself. So it was with the Israelites, as the Midianites were pressing the Israelites on every side trying to drive them from the land of Canaan. They left no substance for Israel and were as grasshoppers for multitude, for both they and their camels were without number (Judges 6:5).

Gideon, a man from the tribe of Manasseh, was pressing wheat by the winepress to hide it from the Midianites and showed all signs of fear and intimidation. God sent an angel of the Lord to encourage Gideon and draft him into His military as the Captain of the Host—for Gideon would smite the Midianites as one man. Gideon wanted a sign from the angel of the Lord, and after the angel performed the sign he departed out of his sight.

When Gideon perceived that he had seen an angel face to face, he feared and acknowledged God saying, "Alas, O Lord God," and build an altar there and called it Jehovah-Shalom. God gave Gideon peace that he could smite the Midianites as "one man"—and so he did with an army of 300 men. God uses crises to reveal His power and strength to His people.

If God can give a nation military peace, He will give the believer emotional peace from the storms of life. Jehovah Shalom means, "The LORD is Peace." The peace of God is confidence, and assurance that we can trust God who is with us in every situation.

The Armor

At this prayer station the believer is encouraged to stand (Ephesians 6:11,13). Standing has a military stance. In means to resist the enemy and hold a critical position in battle. The believer stands therefore with the whole armor of God—and having done all—just stand. Don't turn to the left or the right—by faith believe God and stand, praying always! This is a position where you use *God's word, pray, praise and worship* while *waiting* on Him. "For the battle is not yours but the Lords" (2 Chronicles 20:15).

Moses said unto the people, "fear ye not, stand still and see the salvation of the LORD, which he will show to you today: for the Egyptians whom ye have seen today, ye shall see them again no more forever. The LORD shall fight for you and ye shall hold your peace" (Exodus 14:13-14).

Scripture Reading:

Isaiah 58:6-11 (GNB)

> *The kind of fasting I want is this; Remove the chains of oppression and the yoke of injustice, and let the oppressed go free. Share your food with the hungry and open your homes to the homeless poor. Give clothes to those who have nothing to wear, and do not refuse to help your own relatives. Then my favor will shine on you like the morning sun, and your wounds will be quickly healed. I will always be with you to save you; my presence will protect you on every side. When you pray, I will answer you. When you call to me, I will respond.*

If you put an end to oppression, to every gesture of contempt, and to every evil word; if you give food to the hungry and satisfy those who are in need, then the darkness around you will turn to the brightness of noon. And I will always guide you and satisfy you with good things. I will keep you strong and well. You will be like a garden that has plenty of water, like a spring of water that never goes dry.

Isaiah 1:17-19 (KJV)

Learn to do well; seek judgment, relieve the oppressed, judge the fatherless, plead for the widow. Come now, and let us reason together, saith the LORD: though your sins be as scarlet, they shall be as white as snow; though they be red like crimson, they shall be as wool. If ye be willing and obedient, ye shall eat the good of the land:

Bondage—Focal Point Readings: (KJV)

(Each Prayer Station list specific areas that concern humanity (*focal points*), and are designed to keep the prayer warrior focused while praying and interceding. Focal point scriptures are listed below so that the believer can pray according to the Word of God).

Scripture	Focal Point	Scripture	Focal Point
Psalm 25:18-20, Romans 3:23, Ephesian 4:26	sin, emotional pain, affliction	Romans 8:15, 21	fear, low self esteem
Psalm 32:7		2 Corinthians 2:4	affliction, love
Psalm 119:80	reactive	2 Corinthians 6:3-10	rejection, abuse
Lamentations 1:16	childhood bondage	2 Corinthians 6:14	unequally yoked
Matthew 3:10	generational curses	John 3:16, Galatians 4:19	love of God
Mark 5:2-3	homeless	Philippians 2:3	egoism
John 8:31-36 Philippians 3:4-7	insecurity, culture	Hebrews 12:17	conflict, rejection
Acts 15:36-41	conflict, confusion, unforgiveness	John 9:1-25, James 5:16	relationships, reactive, love of God, childhood bondage
Acts 26:18, 2 Thessalonians 2	illusions, confusion	1 John 4:18	fear
Psalm 62:10, Psalm 119:34	oppression	Acts 4:13, 2 Timothy 2:15	illiterate
1 Samuel 18:6-16, 1Kings 19:9-18, Jeremiah 20:7-13	oppression, depression, insecurity, rejection, emotional pain		

Reflections from the heart: When you reflect on what you have heard it causes you to think about how it has impacted your heart. What changes are you willing to make, or what changes have you made as a result of reflecting? Write down your reflections as you take this journey with the Lord.

Prayer Request: (Be specific!)
(Write out your petition and validate it with scriptures to ensure that it lines up with the Word of God for your life. God's Word is His will!)

Supporting Scriptures:

Date Petition Answered:

ADDICTION

PRAYER STATION XI

"Depart ye, depart ye, go ye out from thence, touch no unclean thing; go ye out of the midst of her; be ye clean, that bear the vessels of the LORD."
(Isaiah 52:11 KJV)

JESUS

Jehovah M'Kaddesh
The Lord who Sanctifies
Leviticus 20:7

Prayer Station XI

Addiction

Romans 8
The Blood of Jesus
Drugs—Crack—Cocaine
Alcohol—Nicotine
Caffeine—Sweets
Medication—Vitamins
Obesity—Anorexia
Co-Dependency
Sexual Devices
Pornography
Cross Dressing
Excessive Shopping
Over Spending—Shopping
Shop Lifting
Gambling
Self Preservation
Television
Lust of Internet—Video Games
Restore Dignity

Stand against the wiles of the Devil

Prayer Station XI—Addiction

Addiction is the result of allowing flesh to be in control, and not walking in the Spirit of God. Jesus calls the flesh "weak" (Mark 14:38). The enemy is trying to use this weakness to destroy the people of God from within by using their own desires against them. Nicotine, caffeine, drugs, food, and alcohol is some of the things of the world that have become an addiction to some people.

We need to strengthen our inner man to take and keep control of our flesh.

Jehovah M'Kaddesh—The Lord who Sanctifies (Leviticus 20:7)

"Sanctify yourselves therefore, and be ye holy: for I am the LORD your God. And ye shall keep my statutes, and do them: I am the LORD which sanctify you" (Leviticus 20:7-8).

Jehovah M'Kaddesh means "the Lord who Sanctifies." Jehovah M'Kaddesh reveals that God is a Holy God. God requires his children to sanctify themselves and to be holy. The believer must sanctify the Lord God in his/her heart in all manner of conversation. In essence, the whole person must be holy.

We have been taught by the Word of God to be holy (I Peter 1:13-16). "And the very God of peace sanctify you wholly; and I pray God your whole spirit and soul and body be preserved blameless unto the coming of our Lord Jesus Christ" (1 Thessalonians 5:23). This should be the prayer of every Christian believer today—to be holy even as God is Holy.

The blood of Jesus can destroy any power of the enemy and can wash the *vilest sinner's* guilt away.

Addition

Some additions involve demonic activity. Not all-mental disorders are demonic. Demon activity can cause physical and mental suffering as well as tempt people to practice immoral habits. These habits can turn into additions. The bible teaches that some people are possessed by demons (Mark 1:23). But God can turn any situation around for our good.

It will take praying, intercession, perseverance and supplication in the Spirit to break the habits of addition. Whenever Jesus comes, all Satan's powers are broken—he will wash your sins away.

The Armor

This station requires the believer to "stand against the wiles of the devil" (Ephesians 6:11). Satan devises schemes and tactics (wiles) against the believer who is to stand fully clothed with his spiritual armor (weapons). The believer under the direction of the Holy Spirit is to intercede for the ungodly until the power of addiction is broken and Christ is formed in them.

Power positions of standing are; praying, worshiping, waiting and faith in the Word of God. It produces perseverance and patience.

"Speaking to yourselves in psalms and hymns and spiritual songs, singing and making melody in your heart to the Lord; giving thanks always for all things unto God and the Father in the name of our Lord Jesus Christ; submitting yourselves one to another in the fear of God" (Ephesians 3:19-21).

The word is a lamp unto my feet and a light in my path—when I can't see my way, the word will provide light. Just stand!

Scripture Reading:

Romans 15:1-4 (GNB)

We who are strong in the faith ought to help the weak to carry their burdens. We should not please ourselves. Instead, we should all please other believers for their own good, in order to build them up in the faith. For Christ did not please himself. Instead, as the scripture says, "The insults which are hurled at you have fallen on me." Everything written in the Scriptures was written to teach us, in order that we might have hope through the patience and encouragement, which the scriptures gives us.

Genesis 9:20-24 (GNB)

Noah, who was a farmer, was the first man to plant a vineyard. After he drank some of the wine, he became drunk, took off his clothes, and lay naked in his tent. When Ham, the father of Canaan, saw that his father was naked, he went out and told his two brothers. Then Shem and Japheth took a robe and held it behind them and their shoulders. They walked backward into the tent and covered their father, keeping their faces turned away so as not to see him naked.

1 Corinthians 6:9-12 (KJV)

Know ye not that the unrighteous shall not inherit the kingdom of God? Be not deceived: neither fornicators, nor idolaters, nor adulterers, nor effeminate, nor abusers of themselves with mankind, nor thieves, nor covetous, nor drunkards, nor revilers, nor extortioners, shall inherit the kingdom of God. And such were some of you: but ye are name of the Lord Jesus, and by the Spirit of our God.

Addition—Focal Point Readings: (KJV)

(Each Prayer Station list specific areas that concern humanity (*focal points*), and are designed to keep the prayer warrior focused while praying and interceding. Focal point scriptures are listed below so that the believer can pray according to the Word of God).

Scripture	Focal Point	Scripture	Focal Point
Deuteronomy 18:10-12	drugs	Romans 6	restore dignity
Proverbs 4:23-27	restore dignity	Romans 7:7-8, 23-25	lust of internet, lust of videos games, television, self preservation
Proverbs 15:27	gambling		
Proverbs 18:9	over shopping	Romans 8	
Proverbs 20:11	internet, video	Romans 12:1-2	restore dignity
Proverbs 21:20	over spending	1 Corinthians 6:12	nicotine, vitamins medication, caffeine
Proverbs 22:6, 15		2 Corinthians 7:10	
Proverbs 23:1-3	obesity, sweets, caffeine	Galatians 5:1, 16-24	self-preservation, pornography, lust, drugs, sexual devices, alcohol, anorexia
Proverbs 23:21	alcohol, obesity	Ephesians 5:1-5	pornography, sexual devices, cross dressing
Proverbs 25:28 , 29:17		Hebrews 2:3	
Proverbs 28:24	shop lifting	Hebrews 13:3-8	
Proverbs 30:12	blood of Jesus		
Romans 1:24	sexual devices, cross dressing		

Reflections from the heart: When you reflect on what you have heard it causes you to think about how it has impacted your heart. What changes are you willing to make, or what changes have you made as a result of reflecting? Write down your reflections as you take this journey with the Lord.

Prayer Request: (Be specific!)

(Write out your petition and validate it with scriptures to ensure that it lines up with the Word of God for your life. God's Word is His will!)

Supporting Scriptures:

Date Petition Answered:

Salvation

Prayer Station XII

"He is astonished to see that there is no one to help the oppressed. So he will use his own power to rescue them and to win the victory. He will wear justice like a coat of armor and saving power like a helmet. He will clothe himself with the strong desire to set things right and to punish and avenge the wrongs that people suffer."
(Isaiah 59:16-17 GNB)

Jesus

Yeshua
God is Salvation
Matthew 1:21

Prayer Station XII

Salvation

John 3:16
KJV
"For God so loved the world, that He gave his only begotten Son, that whosoever believeth in Him should not perish, but have everlasting life."

Romans 5:6
KJV
"For when we were yet without strength, in due time Christ died for the ungodly."

Romans 6:23
KJV
"For the Wages of sin is death; but the gift of God is eternal life through Jesus Christ our Lord."

Romans 10:9
KJV
"That if thou shalt confess with thy mouth the Lord Jesus, and shall believe in thine heart that God hath raised him from the dead, thou shall be saved."

Romans 10:13
KJV
"For whosoever shall call upon the name of the Lord shall be saved."

Acts 4:12
KJV
"Neither is there salvation in any other: for there is none other name under heaven given among men, whereby we must e saved."

Prayer Station XII—Salvation

"That if thou shalt confess with thy mouth the Lord Jesus, and shall believe in thine heart that God hath raised him from the dead, thou shall be saved" (Romans 10:9).

It is God's desire for us as a people to become one (John 17:22, NKJV). What unites the Kingdom of God is the belief that Jesus was sent from heaven to lay down His life for us all (John 10:15).

God's desire is for the world to spend eternity in heaven. Jesus Christ came to show us the way to heaven and provide the miracle of salvation to all. Anyone can receive this gift of God and have everlasting life (John 3:16).

Yeshua—God is Salvation (Matthew 1:21)

The name of Jesus tells much about His character and mission on the earth. The Greek name Jesus comes from the Hebrew name Yeshua, which means "God is Salvation" or "God the Savior." The angel of the Lord revealed to Mary the mother of Jesus that she shall bring forth a son, and thou shalt call his name Jesus: for *he shall save his people from their sins* (Matthew 1:21).

Jesus has many names but only *one name for salvation.*

Some of His names are;

1. Christ, "the Anointed One"
2. Messiah, "the Anointed One"
3. Immanuel "God with us"
4. Master "teacher"
5. Son of God
6. Son of Man

Salvation

Everything the believer needs is in the name of "Jesus"—healing is in the name of Jesus, salvation is in no other but the name of Jesus, deliverance is in the name of Jesus, financial deliverance is in that name, intimacy is in the name of Jesus, everything you need is in the name of Jesus. God revealed Himself in many names in the Old Testament, but in the New Testament all the believer needs is the name of JESUS! Glory be to God.

The number one concern of God is souls. God is not willing that any man should perish, but all come to repentance. His will for man is salvation.

The Armor

There is no armor for this station—at this station the believer is standing fully clothed with the whole armor of God and ready to spoil the strongman's house.

1. Who is the strongman? *Satan*
2. Where is his house? *This world system (world view)*
3. What will the believer spoil or take from the strongman's house? *The souls that belong to God*

The fight is on as the believer leads souls to Christ at Prayer Station XII. Jesus forever lives to make intercession for us—war a good warfare and remember the fight is fixed!

Is soul winning a part of your 5-year plan?

Scriptures Reading:

Leviticus 17:11 (KJV)

> For the life of the flesh is in the blood: and I have given it to you

upon the altar to make an atonement for your souls: for it is the blood that maketh an atonement for the soul.

Hebrews 9:11-14, 22, 24-26 (KJV)

But Christ being come a high priest of good things to come, by a greater and more perfect tabernacle, not made with hands, that is to say, not of this building; Neither by the blood of goats and calves, but by his own blood he entered in once into the holy place, having obtained eternal redemption for us. For if the blood of bulls and of goats, and the ashes of a heifer sprinkling the unclean, sanctifieth to the purifying of the flesh: How much more shall the blood of Christ, who through the eternal Spirit offered himself without spot to God, purge your conscience from dead works to serve the living God?

And almost all things are by the law purged with blood; and without shedding of blood is no remission.

For Christ is not entered into the holy places made with hands, which are the figures of the true; but into heaven itself, now to appear in the presence of God for us. Nor yet that he should offer himself often, as the high priest entereth into the holy place every year with blood of others;

For then must he often have suffered since the foundation of the world: but now once in the end of the world hath he appeared to put away sin by the sacrifice of himself.

Scripture Readings:

Genesis 3
Genesis 7:1, 8:15-19, 9:1
Genesis 12:1-9, 15:1-6
Genesis 18:1-15
Genesis 21:1-8, 22:1-19
Genesis 25:19-34
Genesis 27
Genesis 28, 30, 31, 32, 33, 35
Genesis 37 – 50
Exodus
Matthew 1:18-23
Matthew 26:17-30
Mark 14 - 15 - 16
Luke 22:7-23

Romans 8:3, 5:9
1 Corinthians 11:17-34
2 Corinthians 5:17 Galatians 4:4
Ephesians 1:17
Colossians 1:12-14, 20
Hebrews 9
Hebrews 10:19, 29, 13:12
1 Peter 1 :18-19
1 John 1:7
Revelation 1:5, 5:9 Revelation 12:10, 11
Revelation 22:11, 20

Reflections from the heart: When you reflect on what you have heard it causes you to think about how it has impacted your heart. What changes are you willing to make, or what changes have you made as a result of reflecting? Write down your reflections as you take this journey with the Lord.

Prayer Request: (Be specific!)

(Write out your petition and validate it with scriptures to ensure that it lines up with the Word of God for your life. God's Word is His will!)

Supporting Scriptures:

Date Petition Answered:

Prayer Stations
"On the Run"
for your busy schedule

Jesus

Jehovah Elohim
The Lord Is God
Deuteronomy 10:17

Prayer Station I

Praise and Worship

Psalms 66, 113, 145

Hallow His Name
Holy—Love—Righteous
Faithful—Justice—Mercy
Gracious—Long-suffering
Humble—Goodness
Truth—Forgiving
Omniscience—Omnipotence
Omnipresence—Immutable
Infinite—Wisdom—His Glory
Creator
The Word
Potentate
King of kings—Lord of lords
Majesty—Worthy—Exalted
Alpha—Omega
New Covenant
Atonement—Redemption
Father—Son—Holy Spirit

Whole Armor - Ephesians 6:11-18

Jesus

Jehovah T'Sur
The Lord Our Strength
Psalms 19:14

Prayer Station II

Family

Ephesians 5:22-33

Salvation
Will of God
Love—Unity
Blessings
Communication
Forgiveness
Conflict Resolution
Trust—Stability
Marriage—Singles
Widows—Single Parents
Infidelity—Divorce
Protection—Abuse
Extended Family
Aging Parents—Caregivers
Foster Care
Bereavement
Abortions
Satanic Attacks

Feet Shod with the Gospel of Peace

Jesus

Jehovah Nissi
The Lord Is My Banner
Exodus 17:15

Prayer Station III

Children

Ephesians 6:1-4
Genesis 22:17-18
Salvation
Blessed—Loved—Happy
Stability—Focus—Favor
Wisdom—Integrity
Education—Head not the Tail
Crime—Safety—Protection
Physical—Mental Abuse
Peer Pressure—Adoption
Low Self Esteem—Teen Suicide
Rebellion—Withdrawal
Abstinence—Loneliness Abductions
Incest—Fornication
Child Pornography
Homosexuality
Internet Scams

Helmet of Salvation

Jesus

Jehovah Jireh
The Lord will Provide
Genesis 22:14

Prayer Station IV

Finance

Malachi 3:6-12
Wisdom
Prosperity—Wealth
Tithes—Offerings
Good Stewardship—Faithful
Give and it shall be Given
Honesty—Clean Heart
Jobs—Income—Security
Work Habits
Pledges—Debts Paid
Debts Canceled
Credit Card Debt—Taxes
Debt Free—No Lack
Investments
Stealing- Slothful—Unfaithful
Wages in Bags with Holes
Covert—Pressure—Forgiveness
Outreach—Poor

Loins Girt with Truth

Jesus

Jehovah Rophe
The Lord Who Heals
Exodus 15:26

Prayer Station V

Healing

Isaiah 53, I Peter 2:24-25
Miracles—Signs—Wonders
Mental—Physical—Spiritual
Spirit of Infirmity
Diseases
High Blood Pressure
AIDS
Cancer—Diabetes
Heart—Kidney Disease
Tumors—Arteries
Disorders
Arthritis
Depression
Headaches—Attention Deficit
Gum Disease
Reproductive Failure
Anger—Fear
Grief—Trauma

Shield of Faith

Jesus

El Gibor
The Mighty God
Isaiah 9:6, 10:21

Prayer Station VI

Binding Satan

I John 3:8—Matthew 12:22-32
Mind is the Battlefield
Schemes of the Devil
Cancel His Assignment
Resist Him
Liar—Murderer—Thief
Deceiver—Accuser—Slander
Malice—Hatred
As a Roaring Lion
Atmosphere—Domain
Principalities—Powers
Rulers of Darkness
Spiritual Wickedness
Witchcraft—Disobedience
Unforgiveness
Unbelief—Discord—Blasphemy
Pride—Coveting
Hands that Shed Innocent Blood

**Use your Sword of the Spirit—
The Word**

Jesus

Jehovah Tsidkenu
The Lord our Righteousness
Jeremiah 23:6

Prayer Station VII

Leadership

Romans 13
Family
Churches
Pastor-Spouse
Pastors—Elders—Ministers
Church Leadership
Five Fold Ministry
Laborers for the Harvest
Peace of Jerusalem
Authorities
Neighborhood Watch
County-City-State Government
National Government
President of USA—Nations
Police—Fire Department
Armed Forces
Homeland Security
Employers—Educators
Schools—Colleges—Universities

Breast Plate of Righteousness

Jesus

Immanuel
God with Us
Matthew 1:23

Prayer Station VIII

Unity

John 17
Love of God
Body of Christ
One Body
Many Members
Oneness
That The World May Believe
Mind of Christ
Corporate in Prayer
Prayer of Agreement
Christ Glorified in Us
Cleanse—Sanctify Us
Focused—None be lost
Bearing One Another
Long Suffering
Unity of the Spirit—Faith
Divisions
Rebellion
Binding and Loosing

Praying always with all prayer in the Spirit

Jesus

Jehovah Shammah
The Lord is There
Ezekiel 48:35

Prayer Station IX

Prisoners—Captives

Luke 4:18-19
Salvation
Depravity—Sin
Freedom—Protection
Deliverance from Satan
Undo Burdens—Chains—Fetters
Spirit of Fear—Suicide
Possessed—Oppressive Spirits
Preach the Gospel
Open Prison Doors
Heal the Broken Hearted
Sight to the Blind
Free the Bruised
Dumb Speak—Lame Walk
Wickedness
Oil of Joy for Mourning
Garment of Praise for Heaviness
The Anointing Destroys Yokes

Watching with all perseverance for all Saints

Jesus

Jehovah Shalom
The Lord is Peace
Judges 6:24

Prayer Station X

Bondage

John 8:33-36
Love of God
Sin
Depression
Oppression
Illusions
Insecurity
Confusion—Fear
Abuse—Rejection
Homeless
Unforgiveness
Emotional Pain—Affliction
Low Self Esteem
Egoism—Conflict
Illiterate—Reactive
Unequally Yoked
Relationships—Cultural
Childhood Bondage
Generational Curses

Having Done All to Stand

Jesus

Jehovah M'Kaddesh
The Lord who Sanctifies
Leviticus 20:7

Prayer Station XI

Addiction

Romans 8
The Blood of Jesus
Drugs - Crack - Cocaine
Alcohol - Nicotine
Caffeine - Sweets
Medication - Vitamins
Obesity—Anorexia
Co-Dependency
Sexual Devices
Pornography
Cross Dressing
Excessive Shopping
Over Spending—Shopping
Shop Lifting
Gambling
Self Preservation
Television
Lust of Internet—Video Games
Restore Dignity

Stand against the wiles of the Devil

Jesus

Yeshua
God is Salvation
Matthew 1:21

Prayer Station XII

Salvation

John 3:16—For God so loved the world, that He gave his only begotten Son, that whosoever believeth in Him should not perish, but have everlasting life

Romans 5:6—For when we were yet without strength, in due time Christ died for the ungodly

Romans 6:23—For the Wages of sin is death; but the gift of God is eternal life through Jesus Christ our Lord

Romans 10:9—That if thou shalt confess with thy mouth the Lord Jesus, and shall believe in thine heart that God hath raised him from the dead, thou shall be saved

Romans 10:13—For whosoever shall call upon the name of the Lord shall be saved

Acts 4:12—Neither is there salvation in any other: for there is none other name under heaven given among men, whereby we must be saved

BIBLIOGRAPHY

David Yonggi Cho, Prayer That Brings Revival, Published by Charisma House, 1998

The Names of God, Lester Sumrall, LeSEA Publishing Company, Inc., 1982

Intimately Knowing God Through His Names, Joyce Holmes-Merriman, Bartlett Printing Graphics, 1993

Hebrew-Greek Key Word Study Bible, KJV, Strongs Dictionaries Concordance, Word Studies, AGM Publishers, 1984, Revised Edition 1991

Nelson Study Bible KJV

SUMMARY

Americans of all ages, all stations of life and all types of dispositions are asking for guidelines to focused prayer.

Prayer Stations are not just designated locations where believers go, expecting to receive results from God the Father in the name of Jesus, but are written focal points that keeps the believer focused while praying.

Prayer Stations allows the believer to go outside his/her comfort zones into praying beyond their intellect in the Spirit.

This book allows the believer to study each Prayer Station with supporting scriptures so that they may pray the will of God effectively, keep a written journal and to reflect on how the content of each Prayer Station has impacted their lives.

Prayer Stations can be used also on a professional level in counseling sessions, the dynamics of teams, home devotionals and personal use.

AUTHOR BIOGRAPHY— BYRON R. RAVENELL

Byron F. Ravenell has declared his priority in life is obedience to the will of God. A native of Lawrenceville, New Jersey, a graduate of Ryder University with a BA in Finance. He now resides in Los Angeles California.

AUTHOR BIOGRAPHY— GEORGIA M. HOOD

Georgia M. Hood, an ordained evangelist, called to the will of God. She resides in Princeton, New Jersey a graduate of Philadelphia Biblical University with a BS in Bible and a MS in Christian Counseling.

Printed in the United States
41578LVS00002B/194